LICORICIA
of WINCHESTER

LICORICIA
of WINCHESTER

POWER and PREJUDICE
in MEDIEVAL ENGLAND

The Rise and Fall of a Remarkable
Jewish Businesswoman

by
REBECCA ABRAMS

The Licoricia of Winchester Appeal
Patrons: Simon Sebag Montefiore and Dame Jenny Abramsky DBE
Charity No. 1174453 http://www.licoricia.org

First published 2022
Text © Rebecca Abrams 2022

Paperback ISBN: 978-1-3999-1638-7
Ebook ISBN: 978-1-3999-1791-9

Design and Typesetting: Charlotte Lloyd (charlottelloydemail@gmail.com)
Picture Research: Emily Hedges (emilyhedges.co.uk)

Printed in the UK by Gomer Press

Cover image: Detail of Licoricia of Winchester, sculpture by
Ian Rank-Broadley FRSS. Photo by Iona Wolff, @ionawolffphoto

A note on the type: The typeface used on the cover of this book was created by
Berthold Wolpe, a refugee from Nazism, who settled in England. It is named
Albertus after Saint Albert the Great, a thirteenth century Christian philosopher
and theologian. The typeface used within the text design is Maiola and was
designed by Veronika Burian.

Supported using public funding by

**ARTS COUNCIL
ENGLAND**

LOTTERY FUNDED

Contents

Licoricia's Family Tree

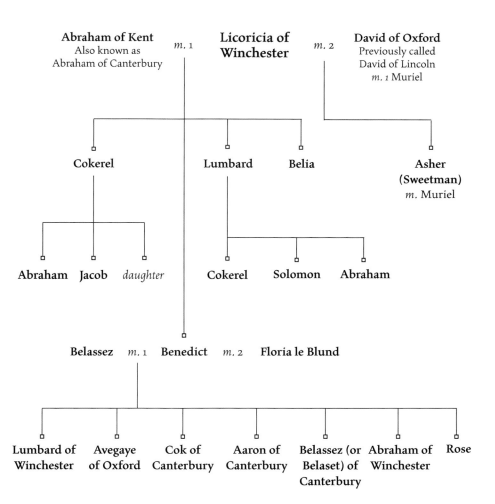

Abraham of Kent
Also known as
Abraham of Canterbury

m. 1

**Licoricia of
Winchester**

m. 2

David of Oxford
Previously called
David of Lincoln
m. 1 Muriel

Cokerel

Lumbard   Belia

**Asher
(Sweetman)**
m. Muriel

Abraham   Jacob   *daughter*

Cokerel   Solomon   Abraham

Belassez   *m. 1*   **Benedict**   *m. 2*   **Floria le Blund**

Lumbard of
Winchester

Avegaye
of Oxford

Cok of
Canterbury

Aaron of
Canterbury

Belassez (or
Belaset) of
Canterbury

Abraham of
Winchester

Rose

A Key to Medieval Monetary Values

	Medieval Sum	Modern Equivalent
1 mark	13s. 4d.	over £500
100 marks	£67	over £50,000
500 marks	£333	over £250,000
1,000 marks	£667	over £500,000
5,000 marks	£3,333	over £2,500,000

Source: Reva Berman Brown and Sean McCartney, 'David of Oxford and Licoricia of Winchester', *Jewish Historical Studies*, 39 (2004).

The above figures are numerical equivalents only and should not be taken as direct financial equivalences, given the profound differences between medieval and modern economies. The only coinage in the reign of Henry III was the silver penny (*denarius* in Latin). There were 240 pennies in a pound and 160 pennies in a mark. A day's wage was around 1d. to 1½d. for a labourer and 24d. for a professional knight. A baron's income could run to several hundred pounds a year, and that of an earl several thousand. A typical annual income for the ruling monarch was around £25,000 a year (from D. Carpenter, *Henry III 1207–1258*, (New Haven and London: Yale University Press, 2020), xv).

Foreword
Simon Sebag Montefiore

This is the biography of a female Jewish potentate in Plantagenet England. You probably will not have heard of her, but she was one of the most important people in the kingdom at the time and this excellent book places her in the centre of history where she belongs. Much history has missed out women and minorities but medieval history in particular is over-populated with a cast of swashbuckling sword-swinging macho barons and kings while Jews too often appear only as victims of massacres and persecution.

As Rebecca Abrams ably elucidates, Licoricia is exceptional – as a Jewish woman who succeeded in acquiring power and wealth – but she is in other ways typical: as a medieval woman and as a Jewish woman, she was inevitably a victim of royal power and a subject of male power. Her biography is remarkable for many reasons: first, she was clearly very able and respected. She became a powerbroker in her own right, lending to King Henry III, Queen Eleanor and to leading clerics and baronial leaders. She was acquainted with king and court. Her payments to the king funded his elaborate renovations of Westminister Abbey, and the building of a magnificent shrine to his patron saint, Edward the Confessor.

Yet for all her success, as Abrams explains in her book, Licoricia was always vulnerable as a member of the Jewish community, a tiny minority that survived under the protection of the monarchy but also at its mercy. Although a few Jews became wealthy, amongst them Licoricia, the vast majority were not richer than anyone else.

Throughout the 13th century Jews in England lived under many repressive rules and restrictions and the recurring menace of violence. The

Crusades which had begun a hundred years before Licoricia's birth were founded on a feverish hatred for infidels, primarily the Moslems who occupied Jerusalem, but also the Jews living innocently in local communities. As Christian kings, barons and mobs of pilgrims set off for the Middle East, they slaughtered Jews in murderous riots across Europe and in England. Jews were also accused of invented crimes based on antisemitic conspiracy theories, most notoriously the Blood Libel which started in England. Many believed that Jews must be forced to convert, or be killed or expelled from Christian kingdoms: all three would take place frequently in the course of Licoricia's lifetime, as this book tragically chronicles.

In many ways Licoricia is a heroine for our time: a woman who thrived in a male world; a commoner who became a powerbroker in a realm of aristocrats and monarchs; a member of a racially-persecuted ethnic minority in an era of murderous racism.

Her story is not just fascinating. In today's world, stalked by clashes between freedom and authoritarianism, racism – including a resurgence of anti-Jewish racism – and intolerance, dark conspiracies and historical facts, Licoricia is enlightening and inspirational for many reasons and such an important and interesting subject for readers today. The erection in February 2022 of a statue in her honour in her home town of Winchester, on the very street where she once lived, is a timely tribute to her life and remarkable achievements in the face of great odds.

Fascinating, tragic and unforgettable, *Licoricia of Winchester: Power and Prejudice in Medieval England* is an untold story of female power, royal intrigue, high finance, civil war and antisemitism. Rebecca Abrams lucidly tells the astonishing rise of Licoricia of Winchester, the richest woman in Plantagenet England, whose unique life and career ended in her murder eight hundred years ago, but who remains in so many ways relevant today.

The statue of Licoricia of Winchester by Ian Rank-Broadley FRSS
in Jewry Street, Winchester

Eschet Chayil   Proverbs 31:10–32

A woman of worth, who can find her? Her price is far beyond rubies.

The heart of her husband trusts her, and no prize does he lack.

She repays him good and not evil all the days of her life.

She seeks out wool and linen and works with willing hands.

She is like merchant ships, from afar she brings her sustenance.

She gets up while it is still night and provides nourishment
for her house and a portion for her maids.

She sets her mind on a field and buys it; from the fruit of her hands
she plants a vineyard.

She girds her loins in strength and gives power to her arms.

She understands that her wares are good; her lamp does not go out at night.

Her hands she reaches out to the distaff, and her palms
hold on to the spindle.

Her palm she opens to the poor, and her hands she extends to the wretched.

She does not fear for her household because of snow, for her
whole household is clothed in scarlet.

Covers she makes for herself; linen and purple, her garments.

Her husband is famed in the gates when he sits with the land's elders.

Fine cloth she makes, and she sells it; a loincloth she gives to the trader.

Strength and grandeur are her garment, and she laughs at the day to come.

She opens her mouth in wisdom; teaching of kindness is on her tongue.

She looks after the ways of her house and does not eat the bread of idleness.

Her sons rise and call her happy, her husband, he praises her:
'Many daughters have done worthy things, but you – you surpass them all!'

Grace is a lie and beauty mere breath; a Lord-fearing woman,
it is she who is praised.

Give her from the fruit of her hands, and let her deeds praise her in the gates.

Translation by Robert Alter

1
INTRODUCTION
Who Was Licoricia of Winchester?

'A woman of worth, who can find her? Her price is far beyond rubies.' So begins the *eschet chayil*, an ancient poem in praise of the ideal woman, composed in the Bronze Age, preserved in the Hebrew Bible, and recited down the generations in Jewish households at the start of the Sabbath.[1] Words and images relating to strength and power run through the poem from top to bottom, conveying both emotional stamina and physical toughness.[2] The 'woman of worth', the poem tells us, is an able businesswoman, as rich in bounty as 'merchant ships', skilled at managing the household finances, able to drive a bargain in the marketplace, plan for the future, and ensure her family is never in material need.

The poem's description is a strikingly good fit for the medieval Jewish busineswoman, Licoricia of Winchester, who lived in England in the thirteenth century.[3] Her first name, Licoricia, comes from the old French word for liquorice, *licoressa*, meaning 'sweet root'. It was an exotic, glamorous and unusual name even in the 1200s, and one that Licoricia more than lived up to, for she was without doubt one of the most extraordinary women of her day.[4]

Twice married and twice widowed, she had at least four sons and a daughter, but her activities, like those of the woman described in *eschet chayil*, extended well beyond the domestic sphere.[5] By the time she was in her early forties, if not before, Licoricia was running a highly successful business as a financier. Her business interests extended over many counties in southern England and brought her into contact with some of the most powerful men and women in the realm, including the king himself, Henry III, with whom she seems to have had an unusually close connection. She would go on to become one of the country's leading financiers and the wealthiest Jewish woman in the whole of England.

Licoricia was connected with several towns and cities in England, including Oxford and Canterbury, but for most of her adult life she lived in Winchester. For more than five decades, the city was her home, her stage and her business headquarters – in short, the epicentre of her world. Her lifetime spanned around seven decades, the reigns of three kings (John, Henry III and Edward I), two civil wars and several attempted foreign invasions, and the events of her own life were as dramatic as the times she lived in. Her first husband was accused of murder, and she was caught up in a high-profile divorce before marrying her second husband, who then died just two years later, leaving her with an infant son and potentially ruinous debts. She was held hostage in the Tower of London on at least four occasions, and she was ready and able, when necessary, to go to court to defend herself and her business interests.

Licoricia's life was powerfully shaped by three factors: the times she lived in, her country, and the fact she was Jewish. Her successes and her setbacks were inextricably connected with those of the Jewish population of England as a whole, both the special status they held and the deprivations they endured. While in many regards her life was not a typical one, her story nevertheless helps to shine light on the wider experiences of English Jews in the thirteenth century. A leading member of the Anglo-Norman Jewry locally and nationally, her rise to prominence reflects the fluidity of the society she lived in and reveals that opportunities for advancement existed for women as well as men.

But financial prosperity and high-ranking connections did not exempt Licoricia from personal sorrows and setbacks and she was vulnerable to many of the same difficulties as other Jews in Norman and Angevin England. She experienced at first-hand the hostility and violence directed at Winchester's Jewish community, including members of her own family, and she herself died in violent circumstances, fatally stabbed along with her maidservant in her home in Winchester in 1277. The killer was never discovered.

In the last decade of Licoricia's life, the English Jewry was subjected to increasingly harsh treatment and physical attacks, and the conditions of

Licorice root from *Herbario Nuovo* by Castore Durante, 1684, Venice

daily life for Jews became ever more fraught with difficulty in the years following her death. Just thirteen years later, on 1 November 1290, Edward I ordered the expulsion of the country's entire Jewish community, amongst them Licoricia's own children and grandchildren.

There is so much about Licoricia of Winchester that we will never know. There are no letters to or from her, no contemporary accounts of her, no known documents bearing her signature and no pictures of her. Most of what we do know about her comes from dry official records written by court clerks, who were not always fully literate in Latin and frequently used different spellings for names and places.[6] Licoricia's own name appears variously as Licor, Licoriz, Licorice and Licoryc. Yet seven and a half centuries on, Licoricia emerges from the historical record as a formidable individual. Courageous, strong-minded and strong-willed, she was an astute and able businesswoman, a powerful matriarch and a leading member of Winchester Jewry. To achieve all she did, as a woman, as a Jew and as a financier in the social, political and religious context of medieval England, she must surely also have been endowed with considerable reserves of resilience, energy, charm and intelligence.

The account of Licoricia's life that follows aims both to answer and to provoke questions about how she accomplished what she did. The thirteenth century world she lived in was remote from our own in many ways; on the other hand, a great many of the challenges Licoricia and the Anglo-Norman Jewry encountered will be familiar to people from many other social, ethnic and religious minorities today. Prejudice and hostility towards those we consider different from ourselves are as much a feature of modern society as they were in the Middle Ages. Now, as then, the root cause is generally fear and ignorance and the result all too often is injustice and cruelty.

In the specific case of prejudice against the Jewish people – 'the longest hatred' as it has been described – the experiences of Licoricia and the Anglo-Norman Jewish community to which she belonged are also instructive. Many elements of modern antisemitism, which saw the murder of over six million Jews in the twentieth century and is still the cause of murderous attacks on individual Jews and Jewish communities around the world in the twenty-first century, can be traced back to the anti-Judaism of the Middle Ages.

Lack of knowledge about how Jews were treated in England in the twelfth and thirteenth centuries matters; it is as unacceptable as the erasure of memories about England's complicity in the slave trade in the eighteenth and nineteenth centuries, or the brutal treatment of the Windrush generation in the twenty-first century. Remembering and learning from the past is our safeguard against repeating the same or similar mistakes in the present and future. Licoricia's story and the wider context of medieval England and medieval Winchester, which so crucially informed and shaped her life, helps us to understand not only her world but our own.

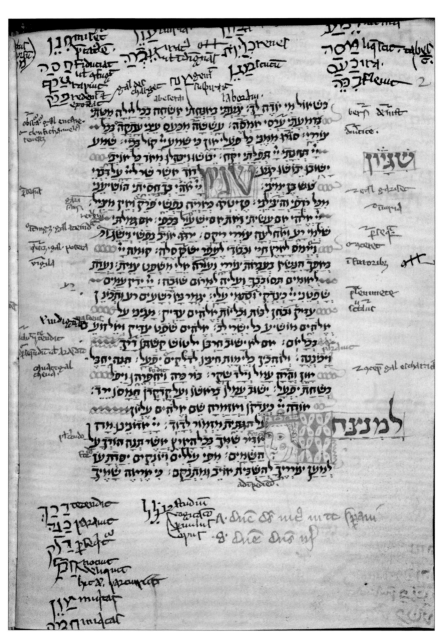

Anglo-Jewish illuminated psalter, Hebrew with Latin and French glosses, mid-13th century,

2

PROTECTION AND PERIL
Being Jewish in Medieval England

By the time Licoricia was born in the early thirteenth century, Jews had been living in England for over a hundred years. They probably first came with the Romans in the first century CE, but there is no firm evidence for their presence until the Middle Ages when they began to settle in England in significant numbers from around 1070, soon after the Norman Conquest.[7] The original members of the medieval Anglo-Jewish community came from Rouen in Normandy at the encouragement of William the Conqueror. Rouennais Jews may even have contributed to William's campaign costs, and in return been enabled by William to settle in England.[8] Later generations of Jews migrated to England from Rouen and other parts of France, Spain, Italy and Germany.[9]

England by the late eleventh century was phenomenally rich in silver and gold plate and high-quality silver coinage, having benefited for decades from the lucrative wool trade with Flanders, silver trade with the Rhineland and trade in luxury goods to and from northern Italy. The conquest of England at a stroke transformed William from the duke of an economically marginal region in northern France into the king of one of the most economically significant coun-

Coin of William the Conqueror, minted in Romney, between 1066 and 1068

Jewish Yeshiva beneath the Palais de Justice, Rouen

tries in western Europe.[10] With Anglo-Saxon merchants initially hostile to the Norman invaders, William probably intended to make use of his Rouen merchants' trading connections and financial skills in the administration of his new kingdom.[11] England was an attractive prospect for the Rouen Jews for similar reasons, offering the chance to expand established trading activities and develop new ones. By the 1130s, this small immigrant community had become one of the most prosperous in Europe, although not from the merchant activities either they or William I had originally envisaged.[12]

Location and population

To begin with, Jews were only permitted to live in London, but during the turbulent reign of King Stephen from 1135 to 1154, they began to settle outside London. By 1189 there were twenty-four major Jewries outside of London, as well as many other smaller communities dotted about the country. The most important Jewish settlements after London were in Lincoln, Canterbury, Northampton, Cambridge, Winchester, Norwich, York, Oxford and Bristol.[13] The links between these communities were always close, and despite later restrictions on where they were allowed to live, Jews frequently moved town and there was regular traffic between the different Jewries, for both business and pleasure. While most of the non-Jewish population in England lived in the countryside, the Jewish community was overwhelmingly urban. Most Christians in the thirteenth century never personally met or knew any Jews.

Over the course of the next hundred years, the fortunes of these provincial communities fluctuated dramatically. More than a few were decimated by local expulsions, physical attacks or poverty long before the mass expulsion of 1290. York Jewry, one of the most prosperous communities by the mid-twelfth century, was almost completely eradicated by the massacre of 1190, yet managed to re-establish itself over the next three decades; the once important Jewish communities of Cambridge and Bristol, on the other hand, were in irreversible decline by the mid-thirteenth century.

Jews only ever constituted a tiny proportion of the overall population, probably around 0.25 per cent (similar to the figure for Britain today). Even

Jewish Communities in Medieval England, 1070–1290

at its peak in around 1240, the Jewish population in England numbered at very most five thousand people out of a total population of around five million. By 1290, their numbers had dwindled to around two thousand.[14] Despite its relative insignificance numerically, the English Jewish community's combined wealth was at times equal to as much as 30 per cent of the country's entire liquid capital.[15]

Taken as a whole, the English Jewry was one of the richest in the whole of Europe, although this does not mean that all Anglo-Norman Jews were rich. Far from it. Most Jewish capital was concentrated in the hands of a very small number of people – probably no more than ten or fifteen families – with the vast majority of Jews no better off than the country's non-Jewish population.[16] Around half of the Jewish population at any one time was too poor to qualify to pay taxes.[17]

Occupations

There were more restrictions in England than elsewhere in medieval Europe on what work Jews were permitted to do, but both men and women were nevertheless engaged in a wide range of occupations within the Jewish community. Some worked as doctors, lawyers and scribes, others as wine and food merchants, metalworkers, jewellers, bakers, butchers, shoe-makers, landlords (and landladies) and peddlers. Jewish women were also employed by Jewish families as midwives and wet-nurses.[18] A small number of Jews who had converted to Christianity worked as royal bodyguards and crossbowmen, as well as dancing tutors and fencing masters to the nobility.[19]

Jewish doctor at the bedside of sick St. Basil. Engraving from a 13th-century German manuscript

One of the occupations open to medieval Jews was lending money at interest, commonly called 'usury' at that time, a term used pejoratively and charged with negative connotations. Usury was officially forbidden to Christians, but Christians always constituted the majority of moneylenders in medieval Europe and operated at all levels of Continental society, despite papal bans and strong disapproval of moneylending.[20] The strong association of Jews with moneylending, which would prove so damaging to Jews in the Middle Ages and long after, was, by contrast, based more on myth and prejudice than reality.[21] While a small proportion were involved in some form of moneylending, the majority of Jews were not moneylenders and, in England as elsewhere, the majority of moneylenders were not Jews.[22]

Historiated letter 'H' depicting Jewish historian Flavius Josephus writing, from Antiquitates Judaicae, 12th century, Netherlandish School

Nevertheless, moneylending and a range of related activities necessary for the economy of medieval England, played a significant role in the extraordinary financial success of the Anglo-Norman Jewry. In the rapidly expanding economy of twelfth-century England, a moneylender was the equivalent of a modern bank, credit card and cashpoint machine combined. Moneylenders, whether Christian or Jewish, performed an increasingly vital function in providing people from all walks of life with access to cash and credit, from the poorest citizens all the way up to bishops, earls, queens and kings. It is no coincidence that the major Jewries outside London in the twelfth century were in towns and cities that were also leading centres for trade and commerce and in most cases hosted major fairs and housed royal mints.[23] It was the creation of regional mints in Stephen's reign that in part facilitated the emergence of the provincial Jewries from the mid-twelfth century on.

Jewish craftsmen working, miniature from Beatae Elisabeth Psalterium, 13th century, Germany

In the pre-banking age of medieval England, wealth was principally held not in cash but in valuable objects, known as 'portables', with gold and silver plate the main way of investing and storing capital. When cash was needed, plate could either be pawned, sold or liquidated. Clothing, jewellery, furs and armour, likewise, could be pawned and sold. Only specially licensed Christian moneyers were allowed to make coin, but there were no restrictions on who could buy and sell plate or exchange foreign coin for English coin.[24] Initially Jewish capital in England came primarily from exchanging currencies and Anglo-Norman Jews up until the 1150s were actively involved in this lively and lucrative trade in foreign coin, gold and silver plate and bullion.[25] Jewish money changers may even have had an edge on their competitors as, unlike Christians, there were no restrictions on where they could travel to do business.[26]

Henry II's reign (1154–1189) brought about a marked shift from money changing to moneylending, in part a consequence of the king's determined efforts to take control of the country's monetary system.[27] From the 1150s on, Jews were increasingly functioning as moneylenders rather than money changers, and by the start of the thirteenth century, tightening restrictions on Christian moneylenders meant that this area of activity was left almost entirely in the hands of Jews.[28]

Jewish men and women, alike, worked as moneylenders, ranging from small-scale pawnbrokers to major financiers. The vast majority were only ever dealing in tiny sums of money, but against this general picture of modest lending, a handful of individual financiers stand out for their remarkable success in building up substantial fortunes through complex portfolios of loans and investments to multiple clients, from middle-class merchants and landowners to the upper echelons of the nobility and top tiers of the clergy.[29]

The most successful of the great Jewish financiers of the twelfth century was Aaron of Lincoln, who was reputedly the wealthiest man in England in his day. When Aaron died in 1186, the Crown confiscated his entire estate and set up a special exchequer to assess the value and extent of his financial assets, a task that took over ten years.[30] Most of the major Jewish finan-

Jewish bankers, from the Cantigas de Santa Maria, 13th century, Spain

ciers were men, but there were at least fifteen significant female financiers in the twelfth and thirteenth centuries, of whom Licoricia of Winchester was one.

Loans in the Middle Ages were not necessarily repaid in cash. They could also be repaid in beer, spices, jewellery and other items. A 'peppercorn rent' was originally quite literally rent paid in pepper, then a high-value commodity. To ensure loans were repaid, they were often secured on items belonging to the person taking out the loan, such as books, clothing, land, buildings, armour and objects made of precious metals. High-ranking clerics at times offered church and cathedral ornaments such as chalices and silver plate as security on their debts, although this was hugely frowned upon by the ecclesiastic authorities.

Loans were nearly always short-term and had to be repaid within a year. Beyond the due date, interest on unpaid debts was typically charged at 2 pence in the pound per week (i.e. 43 per cent a year).[31] This was much less than charges on a modern payday loan and often negotiated down, so it was similar to many credit card interest rates today. Less frequently, the lender would impose a lump sum penalty charge for late payment. Where the loan was secured against revenue, for example from land or property, the revenue itself could be claimed by the lender until the original debt had also been repaid.[32]

By the end of the twelfth century the Crown was taking a much closer interest in Jewish loans and assets.[33] To keep track of these transactions and better protect the Crown's interests in them, the exchequer that had been set up after Aaron of Lincoln died, gradually evolved into the Exchequer of the Jews. From 1196 this functioned as a department of state to record and administer Jewish loans, taxes, fines, inheritance dues and, by extension, to oversee and control the Jewish community itself in a variety of ways.[34] The Exchequer of the Jews was essentially an instrument for state control of Jewish capital, but its remit extended to hearing legal and criminal disputes within the Jewish community and between Christians and Jews.[35] Its only real benefit to the Jews themselves was the provision of a more secure system for registering bonds, collecting debts and settling disputes.[36]

Loans and payments from this time on were typically recorded on chirographs, parchment documents written in Latin and Hebrew and stored in

11th-century Ashkenazi prayer book with handwritten notes in Judeo-Arabic recording loans made by the prayer book's owner to the bishop of Exeter, Bath and Winchester, 11th century

duplicate triple-locked community safes called *archae* (Latin for 'chests'), which were located in important towns.[37] Chirographs were drawn up and witnessed by officially appointed local chirographers, in each case 'two lawful Christians, two lawful Jews and two lawful scribes'.[38] Several hundred of these medieval chirographs have survived, along with a number of Jewish medieval seals.[39]

From the end of the twelfth century, Jewish moneylenders were restricted to living in towns with *archae*, increasing the Crown's ability to monitor its interest in Jewish financial transactions and protect against losses from fire, theft, riots and so forth. When financial disputes arose, as they frequently did, Jews were permitted to bring cases against Christians as well as against each other.[40] The Exchequer of the Jews allowed women as well as men to come to court, regardless of age or marital status. A woman could bring disputes of her own and disputes of a husband or son in which she had an interest.[41] When a husband was accused of breaking the law, a woman could appear as his co-defendant, but when a husband had debts he could not or would not pay, his wife (and children) could be imprisoned in his stead. If the unpaid debt was a tax or fine, the wife had to pay the costs of going to prison out of her own pocket.[42]

The prosperity of the Anglo-Norman Jews between the 1130s and 1240s, especially when compared to many of their Continental co-religionists, was almost certainly a by-product of the social structures of feudal England and the particular ways in which its economy functioned.[43] From the mid-twelfth century, England was unusual both in the extent to which it relied on moneylending and the extent to which high-level lending was carried out by Jews.[44] The English Crown was also unusually active in helping Jews to pursue unpaid loans and interest payments on debts. But the prosperity of the Anglo-Norman Jewish community was always concentrated in the hands of a few individuals, who were in turn dependent on the interests and caprices of the ruling monarch. As the thirteenth century progressed, the particular conditions on which the Jews of medieval England relied for their economic survival became increasingly precarious and, ultimately, as we shall see, evaporated altogether.

Protection and privation

Jews moved to England freely from 1070 on, but they lived in the country under certain conditions, some of which were favourable to them and others not. From the time of Henry II, and possibly before, the Jews were officially granted certain 'liberties and free customs',[45] but they were also the property of the king, along with everything they owned. As the king's possessions, they enjoyed his protection, and they were also vulnerable to his whims.

The Jews' special status was granted in turn by each of the Angevin kings of England: Henry II, Richard, John and Henry III.[46] Jews were allowed to organise and participate in religious worship without interference and live according to their religious laws and traditions. They could travel the king's highways without restraint and were exempt from road tolls. In legal disputes with Christians, they were allowed to represent themselves in court or be represented by a fellow Jew, and they were permitted to swear on the Hebrew Bible or Torah scrolls.. In times of trouble, they could (usually but not invariably) count on royal protection.[47]

This protection, however, was driven almost entirely by royal self-interest. Stealing property from a Jew was tantamount to stealing from the king and in theory there were harsh penalties for anyone who did so. Physical attacks on Jews were seldom punished with much severity, unless significant sums of money were involved. At Richard I's coronation on 3 September 1189 at Westminster Abbey a riot broke out after Jews in the crowd outside were accidentally pushed into the Abbey, unleashing a savage attack on the London Jewry in which at least thirty Jews were murdered in cold blood or died soon after from their injuries. A spate of Jewish massacres in provincial towns followed between January and March 1190.[48] Evidence of many Jewish bonds was destroyed during these attacks, after which the Crown issued new decrees that debts or pledges made to a murdered Jew would immediately become the property of the king, while their killers would be fined or indefinitely imprisoned.[49]

Special status in any case did not mean high status. When the Jews of London complained about harassment early in the thirteenth century, King John wrote to the mayor of London that, as decreed in his 1201 Charter of Liberties to the Jews, the Jews must not be harmed, reminding the mayor that 'if we give our peace to a dog it ought to be preserved inviolate'.[50] In other words, even the lowest of the low had to be treated well if the king of England so commanded. King John also viewed torturing Jews as entirely acceptable when he saw fit.

Royal protection came at a high price: in return, the king expected regular financial gifts, known as *donums*. These were not really gifts at all but random demands for money, which were 'imposed at the king's will and could not be refused'.[51] By the latter stages of the twelfth century this had evolved into a system of taxes known as tallages, for which all Jews

Four Kings of England: Henry II, Richard I, John and Henry III from The Kings of England from Brutus to Henry III, by Matthew Paris, c. 1250–59

over the age of twelve, male and female, were liable. The amount paid by each Jewish community varied and was negotiable, depending on the combined wealth of its inhabitants, and was paid according to their individual means. In 1221, half of the entire Winchester tallage was paid by just one family, that of the Jewish businesswoman Chera of Winchester.

Tallages were generally paid every three or four years, although this varied according to the financial need and greed of the ruling monarch. How the individual Jewries raised these sums was up to them, but punishment for non-payment was harsh. Leading members of the community (or members of their family) could be imprisoned and held hostage for weeks until the sums were paid. On several occasions, entire communities were locked up, including women and children.

In addition to the regular tallages, the Jews were also frequently ordered to pay heavy one-off taxes. In 1210, the rapacious and brutal King John, who had just returned victorious but broke from an expensive military campaign in Ireland, imposed a tallage on the Jews for a staggering £40,000. No Jew, however poor, was exempt. When the money could not be raised, Jewish property and bonds were seized by the Crown, and many individuals were imprisoned and horribly tortured, or fled the country.

King John's tallages destroyed whole Jewish communities and 'a generation of Jewish leaders was wiped out through death, flight or execution'.[52] But John was by no means the first or last of the English kings to make ruthless financial use of the Jews, or to disregard the impact this had on the Jews themselves. In Licoricia's lifetime, Henry III regularly resorted to the same method to raise money for military campaigns, to keep allies on side and to appease troublesome knights and barons. It has been estimated that the Jews contributed between one seventh and one tenth of royal income in the thirteenth century.[53]

Tallages were in effect a form of indirect taxation, since often the only way for the Jewry to raise the large sums of cash demanded by the king at short notice was to call in debts from their Christian clients, who were often equally hard-pressed to find the money required. This practice therefore did little to promote amicable relations between Christians and Jews, however useful it may have been as a means to replenish the royal coffers.

Anglo-Norman Jews were also subject to a raft of legal restrictions. They were not allowed to leave the country, remarry, or carry a corpse over a bridge, for example, without paying for permission to do so. For their first hundred years in England, Jews were forbidden to bury their dead anywhere other than in London, no matter where in the country they lived. This must have caused bereaved Jewish families considerable distress since, even in fair weather, the journey to London along rough medieval roads and tracks would have taken anything from days to weeks, making it virtually impossible for Jews outside London to observe their funeral customs, which required burial within twenty-four hours of death.[54]

From 1177, Henry II granted the Jews permission to have cemeteries in the provinces, as long as these were situated outside the city walls, but even then it was forbidden to carry a Jewish corpse through the Christian city. In Oxford, the circuitous funeral route that medieval Jews were obliged to take from the Jewish quarter in the city's centre to their cemetery beyond the city boundaries still exists and to this day is known as Dead Man's Walk.

The Jews and the Church

Restrictions on burial customs were part and parcel of a range of repressive rules endured by the Anglo-Norman Jews during their two hundred years in England, restrictions that became markedly more numerous and problematic in the course of the thirteenth century. The term 'antisemitism' was not coined until the nineteenth century, but anti-Jewish sentiment was widespread in medieval England as it was throughout Christian Europe, much of it driven by the Church. For most of the thirteenth century, Jews were officially forbidden to make noise audible from outside during their religious services, banned from hiring Christian servants and from eating and drinking with Christians. They were not permitted to touch food sold on Christian market stalls and had to use a stick to point to what they wanted to buy. Prohibitions became increasingly severe as the century progressed and by the mid-1270s Jews were banned from selling their bonds, buying properties unless for their own use or to rent to other Jews, and ultimately from any form of moneylending.

One of the most egregious rulings, introduced in the early thirteenth century was that Jews had to identify their Jewishness visibly by wearing the '*pileum cornatum*', a pointed conical-shaped hat, or the '*tabula*', a cloth badge stitched on to their clothing, the 'badge of shame' as Jews called it. This ruling, which originated from the Lateran Council in Rome and applied throughout Christian Europe, was intended to make Jews more easily distinguishable from Christians as 'a prevention against miscegenation'.[55]

One of a raft of anti-Jewish rulings issued by the Pope between 1179 and 1215, the obligation for Jews to wear the badge on their outer garments was formally adopted in England in 1222 at the Oxford Synod. This took the form of two white strips of linen or parchment, representing the two tablets of the Law, given by God to the Hebrew prophet Moses on Mount Sinai, on which were carved the Ten Commandments.

Jews wearing badges, detail from the Rochester Chronicle, 14th century

The 1222 Oxford Synod also banned Jews from building new synagogues in places they were not already settled, buying or eating meat during Lent, entering churches, making excessive noise during their religious worship, or hiring Christian women as servants and wet-nurses.[56] Although not implemented with much vigour until the 1250s, these rulings marked the start in England of a more oppressive and hostile attitude towards Jews, which would become steadily worse as the century progressed. From 1275 on, all Jews over the age of seven, both girls and boys, had to wear the badge, which had to be yellow in colour, measure 15cm by 1.5cm, and be attached to outer garments and clearly visible.

Official edicts banning or imposing certain activities, however, often indicate that the exact opposite was taking place. Despite the prohibitions, monks in the late thirteenth century complained about 'continuous ululations' from Jews praying in the synagogue next door to their church.[57] There are likewise accounts of Christians continuing to buy food from Jews and partaking with gusto in Jewish wedding festivities as late as 1286, despite the risk of excommunication.[58] Jews could, and often did, pay not to wear the identifying badge.[59] In 1221 the Oxford Jewry, for example, paid 4s. 6d. for permission not to wear the badge. The Winchester Jewry did likewise. Some Jews, including Licoricia, were still employing Christian servants as late as the 1270s.[60]

While some of these restrictions ostensibly served some kind of financial purpose (from the Crown's point of view), many others reflected or promoted theological attitudes and prejudices that were unapologetically anti-Jewish. The ban on Jews touching Christian food, for example, was underpinned by the idea that Jews were spiritually and physically impure and unhealthy, and linked to a belief widely held by non-Jews that Jewish men menstruated and Jewish women were uncontrollably lustful. In a different twist on the same theme, the chronicler Gerald of Wales in *Jewel of the Church* put forward the idea that not eating pork made Jews more appealing to the Devil. Gerald relates how a demon in Italy had told him this personally.[61]

By far the most pernicious manifestation of anti-Jewish prejudice in the Middle Ages was the unfounded accusation that Jews secretly used the blood of Christian children in their religious rites. These accusations (now known as the 'blood libel') originated in medieval England. The first recorded blood libel occurred in Norwich in 1144, and although no evidence was ever found to support the accusation – the murderer was in fact a Christian – there were recurrent child murder accusations against Jews in England from then on, for example in Gloucester in 1168, Bury St Edmunds in 1181, and Lincoln in 1255.[62] In Winchester alone, Jews were falsely accused of child murder in 1192, 1225, 1232 and 1235. Ritual murder accusations emanated from medieval England, but were not confined either to England or to the Middle Ages. They provoked, or were used to justify, physical violence against Jews

Jew from the wall of the Holy Sepulchre Chapel, Winchester Cathedral, depicted wearing the *pileum cornatum*, 12th century

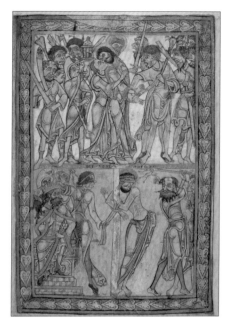

The betrayal of Jesus. Winchester Psalter (Psalter of Henry of Blois, Psalter of St. Swithun Winchester, between 1121 and 1161)

throughout Christian Europe for the next seven centuries, up to and including the Nazi Holocaust in the twentieth century.[63]

Images in stained glass, wall paintings, manuscript illustrations and statuary all helped to reinforce negative beliefs and caricatures associated with Jews.[64] In Winchester Cathedral, twelfth century wall paintings in the Chapel of the Holy Sepulchre contain depictions of Jews wearing the *pileum cornatum*, or pointed hat.[65] A picture in the Winchester Psalter from c.1150 depicts Jews as 'hideous monsters ... with grotesque faces, sharp teeth and enormous moustaches', watching Jesus's suffering with evident glee.[66] Long after the Jews had been expelled from the country, negative images of Jews and Judaism continued to express and embed anti-Jewish sentiment and beliefs.[67] Sixteenth-century wall paintings in the Lady Chapel of Winchester Cathedral include the story of 'The Jew of Bourges', in which a Jewish boy who has taken holy communion is thrown into a heated oven by his father but is then rescued unharmed by the Virgin Mary. The story links Jews with anti-Jewish

Legend of the Jew of Bourges, East end, Winchester Cathedral, early 16th century

myths of child murder and host desecration.[68] Stained glass in Lincoln Cathedral and Norwich Cathedral carried similarly hostile messages.

Anti-Jewish sentiment in medieval England was seeded in Christian teaching, which cast Jews as infidels and the killers of Jesus. From the mid-twelfth century on, the Christian Crusades further fuelled social and religious antipathy towards Jews. Richard I's preparations to go on Crusade in 1190 stoked a hostile atmosphere towards Jews that led to the violent attacks on the Jewries in 1189–90, the worst of which was in York, where in March 1190 the entire Jewry was wiped out in the space of a few days.

The Church was not the only source of antisemitism in medieval England. Throughout the thirteenth century, hostility towards Jews was further fanned by resentment towards Jewish moneylenders and increasing antipathy towards foreigners generally and the Norman ruling elite in particular, with which the Jewry was closely associated because of its own Norman origins and ongoing links with France.[69] Jews in medieval England were thus triply tainted: as infidels, as moneylenders and as foreigners. Whenever political, social and economic tensions ran high, Jews were easy scapegoats and Jewish lives were invariably at risk.

Jewish education and culture

Regardless of the difficulties they faced, the Anglo-Norman Jewish community nevertheless continued to thrive and prosper in many ways, most notably in its intellectual and religious activities. The Middle Ages in general were a vibrant time for Jewish scholarship throughout Europe and the Near East, and intellectual learning was highly revered. This was the age of the great medieval rabbis, Rashi (1040–1105) in France, and Maimonides (1138–1204) in Spain and North Africa. The English Jewry, too, included many outstanding scholars, from Rabbi Josce of London in the early twelfth century to Jacob ben Judah of London in the late thirteenth century.

The challenge of keeping Jewish customs and traditions alive in an overwhelmingly non-Jewish and sometimes overtly hostile context prompted medieval Jewish authors to come up with guidance and 'practical solutions for the situations in which they found themselves'.[70] Berachiah haNaqdan, dubbed 'the Jewish Aesop', probably came to England from Rouen and settled in Oxford in the mid-twelfth century, where he wrote a series of animal fables, several of which appear to contain coded messages to his Jewish readers about how to navigate the complex world of Angevin England.[71] *The Tree of Life (Etz Hayyim)* by Jacob ben Judah was a detailed compendium of Jewish ritual codes for the festivals and high holy days tailored to the Jews living in England. Three poems by Jacob have also survived. Another Jewish poet forged on the rocky ground of late thirteenth-century England was Meir ben Elijah of Norwich, whose powerful *piyyutim* (liturgical poems) articulate the despair of 'a generation on the brink of oblivion'.[72]

Compared to the general population of England, the Jewish community was highly literate. Boys were educated from the age of five or six up to thirteen, and many girls also were taught to read and write. As a student of the Catholic priest Peter Abelard remarked: 'A Jew, even if he is poor, if he has ten sons, will make them all study their letters, not for gain as Christians do, but so they can learn God's law; he will teach not only his sons to read, but his daughters too.'[73] This was in part because study of the Hebrew Bible (which broadly corresponds to the Christian Old Testament) as well

Children's writing book from the Cairo Genizah, 11th-13th century

as rabbinic and Talmudic texts was a central part of Jewish culture and religion, and a vital way to keep Jewish culture and customs alive. Being able to read these texts required knowledge of both Hebrew and Aramaic. The ability to read and write in Norman-French, and to a lesser extent Latin, was also important 'for legal purposes, commercial purposes and in daily life', since the Jews' survival as a community relied upon financial transactions that had to be documented and managed, read and written.[74]

Evidence of Jewish literacy in medieval England has survived in religious manuscripts, poetry, bonds, seals, receipts, petitions, licences, land and property leases, and pledges. Books and documents produced by English Jews also offer glimpses into the intellectual richness of Jewish life.[75] In his important work of linguistics, the *Sepher ha-Shoham*, Moses ben Isaac ha-Nessiah of London drew on a wide range of Sephardic texts and earlier authorities, revealing the international scope of the literature and learning available to English Jews in the thirteenth century.[76]

Many of these important scholars played leading civic roles in the Jewish community. Rabbi Josce was the head of the original London community and probably founded the *magna scola*, which was closely modelled on the synagogue in Rouen. A great scholar and businessman, Rabbi Josce continued to have financial interests in Normandy and kept a large house in Rouen. One of Josce's friends was the brilliant Sephardic scholar Abraham ibn Ezra, who stayed with Josce when he visited London in 1158. A century later the eminent grammarian and lexicographer Master Moses of London (d. c. 1268) was Master of the Law for the community and a senior figure on the English *Bet Din* (the ruling council of the Anglo-Jewry), which in 1242 was to play a critical role in Licoricia's life. A manuscript containing Master Moses' guidelines on legal issues, including marriage and divorce, survives today in the collections of the Bodleian Library in Oxford.[77]

A book in medieval England could cost the same as a house, and Hebrew books were consequently valuable and prized possessions.[78] The Jewish magnate David of Oxford, who became Licoricia's second husband, was a keen collector and built up a valuable library of books, three of which the king took for himself after David's death. When the Jews were driven out of England in 1290, the Benedictine monk Bartholomew Cotton reported that they left '*una cum libris suis*', each one with his book.[79]

Many Christian scholars in medieval England were also interested in Hebrew texts and Jewish knowledge, and there is evidence of Christians working with Jewish scribes and scholars to make translations of Hebrew texts.[80] A Hebrew manuscript made in England in the thirteenth century, for example, now in the Bodleian Library, was painstakingly glossed in both Anglo-Norman and Latin,[81] while a surviving thirteenth-century Hebrew prayer book, written by and for use by Jews, contains copious notes about vocabulary and grammar added to the margins in French and Latin.[82] Hebrew manuscripts that had been taken, borrowed or bought from Jews before and immediately after the 1290 expulsion were still being studied by Christian Hebraists in England many centuries later.[83]

An evolving community

In the course of the two hundred years from the arrival of the Jews from Rouen and elsewhere soon after 1066 to the mass expulsion in 1290, the Jewish community changed and evolved, and conditions for the Jews were very different at different times. In their daily lives, Jews were never segregated from their Christian neighbours, either socially or physically. They lived cheek by jowl in the same streets, shopped at the same market stalls, enjoyed friendships with one another, worked together, ate and drank together, quarrelled with one another, and helped each other out.[84] Although never great in number, they were nevertheless generally tolerated by and embedded in the towns and cities in which they lived. Their position within these Christian medieval communities was in some ways analogous to that of Jewish innkeepers in the Russian empire in the eighteenth and nineteenth centuries: seen by non-Jews as 'other' and different, but also, for the most part, accepted and useful. In both cases, peaceful times ensured a degree of stability for Jews, but when the economic balance of power was upset, as it was by the civil wars in England in the thirteenth century and the emancipation of the serfs in Russia in the nineteenth century, their position quickly became precarious.

Even in turbulent times, however, there were cases of Jews and Christians coming to each other's assistance. In 1187, when Christ Church Cathedral in Canterbury was under attack from the hostile forces of Archbishop

Anglo-Jewish book of Ezekiel, in Hebrew with interlinear Latin translation and the Latin Vulgate text on the margin. Early 13th century

Baldwin, local Jews not only smuggled food to the monks trapped inside the cathedral, but prayed in the cathedral for the monks' safety.[85] At other times Christians provided refuge for imperilled Jews in their monasteries, castles and prisons. There are even examples of Christians converting to Judaism in order to marry, although intermarriage was unusual and strongly discouraged by both religions.[86]

Life in medieval England was never straightforward for Jews. Granted freedoms that Christian subjects were not, they were at the same time vulnerable in ways that Christians were not; toleration and persecution were both realities for English medieval Jews. While they were only ever a small social minority in England, they were by no means socially isolated, retaining close connections with other Jewish communities in England, France and across northern Europe. Through their activities in trade, finance, law and religion, they also frequently came into contact with non-Jews from many places in and far beyond the city. Anti-Jewish sentiment was never far below the surface of Christian medieval England, but set against instances of horrifying flare-ups of violence, there were also settled periods of largely peaceful co-existence. But the thirteenth century saw a decisive and negative shift in the official treatment of England's Jews from protection to restriction and from privilege to precarity, in the form of new regulations that emanated from and were increasingly enforced by the Crown and the Church.[87] This, then, was the complex and contradictory context into which Licoricia of Winchester was born and within which she lived her life.

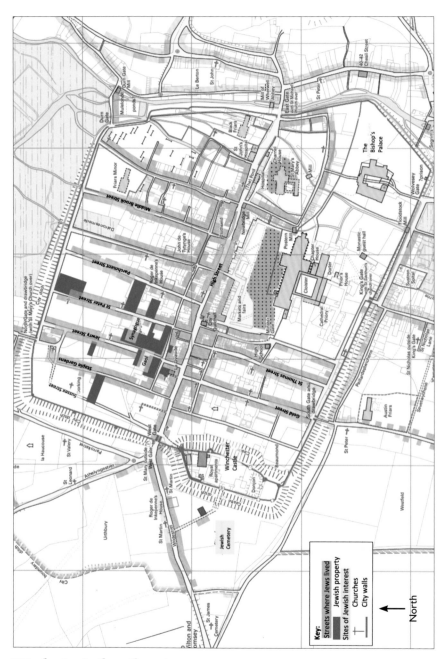

Winchester in the 13th century

After Map 6, *Winchester* c. 1300, first published in the British Historic Towns Atlas Volume VI, *Winchester* © Historic Towns Trust and Winchester Excavations Committee 2017; not to be reproduced without written permission of copyright holders.

3
WINCHESTER
The City and the Jewry

Licoricia's remarkable story cannot be understood without taking into account the city in which she spent most of her life. No visitor to Winchester in the thirteenth century could have doubted the city's status and prosperity. Dominating the skyline, the scale and grandeur of the castle and cathedral would have made this immediately apparent. A major centre since as early as the Roman invasion in the first century CE, Winchester, also known as Winton, was the capital city of Anglo-Saxon England until the Norman Conquest in 1066; the bones of the Anglo-Saxon rulers King Cnut, Queen Emma and William Rufus are to this day said to be housed in mortuary chests in the cathedral. Under the Norman monarchs, London became the capital, but Winchester remained one of England's wealthiest and most powerful cities for the next two hundred years.[88] During the twelfth century, it continued to be the financial centre of England, housing both the royal exchequer and the treasury, and the Winchester mint was the most prestigious in England after London until around 1180, when the mint house burned down.

The first Norman kings and bishops quickly stamped their physical mark on the city by sweeping away the sites of Anglo-Saxon power and replacing them with impressive buildings in the Norman style: a huge new castle, covering 4 per cent of the city's total area; a massively expanded royal palace, nearly equal in size to the Palace of Westminster; and a magnificent new cathedral, four times bigger than the one it replaced and the second-largest church in the whole of western Europe.[89] Wolvesey Palace, chief residence of the bishops of Winchester, was also rebuilt and greatly expanded in the twelfth century, turning it into the 'largest non-monastic domestic building in England' after the Great Hall at Westminster.[90]

The castle was seriously damaged during the civil war between Stephen and Matilda (1138–53), and although Henry II, their agreed heir, made substantial repairs and improvements to the castle, he only occasionally visited the city, and more often for leisure than state business. As royal presence in the city declined, the Church filled the vacuum.[91] Besides the stunning Norman cathedral, there were myriad other religious buildings and institutions. By 1150, there were as many as fifty-seven parish churches, as well as St Mary's Convent, St Swithun's and Hyde Abbey, and two religious hospitals, St Cross (1136) and St Mary Magdalen (1148), each with their own residential buildings, refectories, chapels and physic gardens.

Winchester held its own as a southern powerhouse in the thirteenth century thanks in large part to Henry III.[92] Born in Winchester Castle in 1207, Henry was greatly attached to the city and spent as much time there as possible throughout his long reign.[93] An 'amiable, easy-going, and sympathetic' character, Henry preferred hosting lavish feasts and relaxing with his family at his various castles to the exertions of hunting, joust-

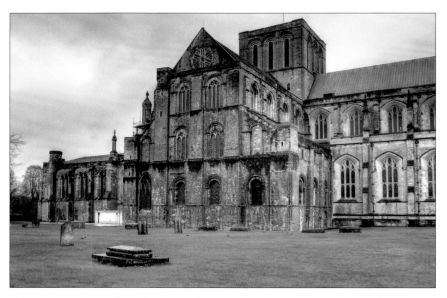

Winchester Cathedral showing the Norman north transept familiar to Licoricia

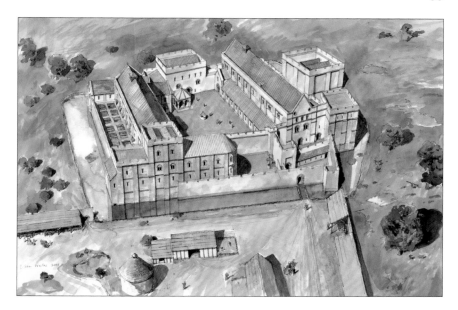

Reconstruction drawing of the Old Bishop's Palace, later known as Wolvesey Castle, c. 1170

ing and fighting, and was notorious for his explosive temper and political vacillation. Ostentatiously pious, he attended mass daily and gave generously to the poor and the Church, although his Christian devotion also contained a deep strain of antisemitism. His secular passions were art and architecture, and he spared no expense in renovating his favourite castles and palaces at Westminster, Windsor, Lincoln, Dover and Winchester. In the 1230s, he 'rebuilt, remodelled or redecorated' virtually every room and building in the Winchester Castle complex, the favourite of all his royal residences, and expended no less than £10,000 transforming it into a palace fit for a king.[94] For all these projects, Jewish taxes were a regular and necessary source of funding.

Straddling the ecclesiastical and royal spheres in Winchester in the first three decades of the thirteenth century was the powerful and controversial figure of Peter des Roches, who served as Lord Chamberlain under Richard I, and was Bishop of Winchester from 1206, Chief Justiciar (the most senior political and legal officer of England) from 1213, and Sheriff of Hampshire from 1216. As King John's right-hand man, Peter des Roches was instrumental in designing and extracting punishing tallages from the

The tomb of Peter des Roches, 13th century, Winchester Cathedral

Jews early in John's reign.[95] From 1217, after the First Barons' War, the entire English Jewry came under des Roches's control in his role as Henry III's guardian, until the young king came of age in 1220.[96]

Des Roches was one of the richest bishops not just in England but the whole of Europe. Consecrated in Gloucester Cathedral rather than Westminster (because London was then in the hands of Prince Louis of France), des Roches was born and raised in France, a fact frequently referred to by his detractors.[97] Dubbed the 'warrior bishop', des Roches started out as a soldier and never lost his taste for physical adventure. He kept a contingent of knights at Winchester, took part in campaigns against rebel forces in Wales, Ireland and Scotland, and reputedly played a decisive role in King John's victory over the French at the Battle of Lincoln in May 1216. Intensely loyal to King John, he deputised for the king in his absence and was tutor and guardian to his eldest son and heir, Henry. After John's death in 1216, des Roches was for over a decade one of Henry III's most trusted and influential advisors.

Whether he was 'hard as rock' in the negative view of the monks of Winchester, or 'a firm rock' in the favourable view of the canons of the abbey that he founded at Titchfield, des Roches was a skilled politician and courtier, who for more than thirty years was deeply involved in affairs of state and the Church at a national and international level.[98] He brokered agreements between emperors and popes (1230), and between England

and France (1231), and until he fell from royal favour in 1234 he was no less important at a local level.[99]

As Bishop of Winchester, he greatly expanded the wealth and power of the Winchester See (the area falling under his jurisdiction). In 1231 he created a large swathe of self-governing, Church-owned land in Winchester called the Soke,[100] founded more than a dozen monasteries in England and France, and was instrumental in helping the Dominican friars come to Winchester. He also led the revival in Anglo-Saxon shrines, including St Swithun's in Winchester.

Des Roches' local power and influence extended for many years over virtually every aspect of daily life in Winchester. His often unscrupulous methods of land acquisition typically involved squeezing out cash-strapped local landowners, and he made frequent use of Winchester's Jewish moneylenders to secure these financial transactions.[101] Admired and loathed in equal measure, he earned the hostility of many local landowners by his ruthless means of acquiring land, achieved in part through his close associations with Jewish financiers.[102] His actions were by no means always favourable to the Jews, but as long as they were useful to him, des Roches was something of an ally for the Jewish community in and beyond Winchester.

The Winchester Jewry

Within this profoundly Christian landscape nestled the Winchester Jewry. Many of the political and ecclesiastical battles of the thirteenth century played out a stone's throw from Licoricia's house in Scowrtenestret, or Shoemakers Street, now called Jewry Street. The castle and cathedral, the physical and symbolic hubs of power, were just a short walk from her front door. The constant din of stonemasons, carpenters and builders hard at work in the compact medieval city would have been audible reminders of precisely where power lay and in whose hands. News, too, would have travelled quickly in this densely populated and close-quartered society.

Jewry Street was home to many of Winchester's Jews from the mid-twelfth century on. Officially renamed Jewry Street in 1302, after the

Jews had been driven out of England, it was probably already known by that name informally.[103] A busy thoroughfare then as now, Jewry Street was an important north-south axis through the city, running from the North Gate to the High Street, and one of the main routes leading to the city's commercial centre where the Guildhall was located and local markets were held. In the north suburb and south of Jewry Street were Hyde Abbey and the Cathedral Priory, respectively, both of which did business with the Winchester Jews in the thirteenth century.

Medieval Jewish token (obverse) found in excavations at Lower Brook Street, Winchester in 1968

Token BS sf 3154, © Winchester Excavations Committee 2012; not to be reproduced without written permission of copyright holder.

Jews known to have lived on Jewry Street include Abraham Crespin and his wife Flora; Chera of Winchester and her sons, Deulebene and Abraham Pinche; Licoricia's sons Cokerel, Lumbard and Benedict; Samarian, son of Lumbard; Isaac of Southwark; Isaac of Newbury; Jospin, son of Gloria; Samarian the Jew; and Abraham, son of Elias. At the time of the 1290 expulsion, Licoricia's grandson, Jacob, son of Cokerel, had two properties (known as 'messuages') on Jewry Street.

Most ordinary houses were made from timber posts set in foundation pits, but the houses of wealthier individuals, including Jews, were built of stone, often with sizeable

Jew's House, Lincoln, one of the earliest extant town houses in England. It is situated on Steep Hill. The house has traditionally been associated with the Jewish community in Medieval Lincoln

plots of land attached.[104] There were no ghettos in medieval England, and unlike other parts of Europe, Jews were not restricted to particular streets or areas, or exclusive to them until the last quarter of the thirteenth century, although Jews often chose to live close to one another, thus creating unofficial Jewish districts.[105] Only in 1275 did the English Crown impose restrictions on Jewish living arrangements, when for the first time it was decreed that 'no Christian, for this Cause or any other, shall dwell among them [Jews].'[106]

In Winchester, certainly until 1275 and quite possibly even after, Jews lived side by side with Christians in many parts of the city, including Brudernestrete (now Staple Garden); Fleshmongerstrete (St Peter's Street); Parchmentstrete (Parchment Street); Wongarstrete (Middle Brook Street), which lay parallel to Jewry Street; Wodestrete (Romsey Road); the High Street, the major route running from the East Gate to the West Gate; Goldstrete (Southgate Street); and Calpestrete (St Thomas Street), which lay between the castle and the cathedral and ran down to the city's southern boundary.

Licoricia's eldest son, Cokerel, had a house in what is now Southgate Street, and her second son, Benedict, who became a major financier in his own right, owned several properties in the city, including a house at the southern end of what is now St Peter's Street, and another much larger house at its northern end, close to the city wall and backing on to or connected to a house on Parchment Street. He also owned property beyond the East Gate, close to the Durn Gate and conveniently near to the Fishbed and the Durn Gate Mills.

The synagogue

The Winchester synagogue was situated behind a house on the eastern side of Jewry Street. Known in medieval England and France as the *scola* (school), the synagogue was the religious heart of the Jewish community, serving as both the *Bet Tefilah* (House of Prayer), where religious worship took place, and the *Bet Midrash* (House of Study), where adult learning took place and where children were educated. In medieval England, as elsewhere in Europe, making sure there was somewhere to pray and study was a top priority for every Jewish community, a responsibility that usually fell to leading members of the Jewry.[107]

English Jews broadly followed the medieval precursors of the religious rites used by Ashkenazi Jews today.[108] Men went to synagogue to pray three times a day, for *shacharit* in the morning, *mincha* in the afternoon, and *maariv* in the evening. Medieval women were under no religious obligation to attend synagogue for prayers and probably did so much less frequently and probably only on the morning of the Sabbath, which lasts from Friday evening to Saturday evening. Men and women did not worship together but in adjoining rooms.

The synagogue was also the heart of the community's social life. This was where people gathered for all kinds of communal events from wedding celebrations to disciplinary hearings. Kitchens, wells and ovens were frequent features of a synagogue, to ensure that food and drink were prepared according to *kashrut* (Jewish religious dietary rules). Meat and poultry also had to be slaughtered in line with the rules of *kashrut*.

In contrast to the confident displays of Christianity on view everywhere in medieval England, the synagogue was usually tucked away out of sight, typically inside, underneath or behind a domestic property, ensuring worshippers both privacy and a degree of safety. In Guildford, the small twelfth-century synagogue, discovered during excavations in 1995, was situated below street level. Scorch marks in an alcove in the east of the room may have been made by the flame of a ritual candle, or *Ner Tamid* (Everlasting Light). A Jewish property in twelfth-century Nottingham also contained a *scola*, which was situated in a cellar or crypt accessed through the main building and rented to the local Jewish community. Jacob's Hall in Oxford, which in the thirteenth century was the home of Jacob of Oxford, contained a vaulted stone cellar, which may have served as a *scola* or *yeshiva* (a centre of Jewish learning).[109] Religious services could be held anywhere as long as there were at least ten Jewish men present, so in some cases the *scola* would simply have been a room within a private property.[110]

The Winchester Jewry could afford a separate building for its synagogue, and by the 1230s this lay behind a house on Jewry Street belonging to the family of Chera of Winchester, whose eldest son, Deulebene, was master of the synagogue.[111] After Deulebene died in 1235, his brother Abraham

Pinche took over this role. Three years later, Abraham was charged with theft and executed, whereupon his house and belongings were confiscated. The Jewry tried its best to argue that the synagogue was not part of the Jewry Street house, but was overruled by the king, who added insult to injury by giving it to one of his castle cooks. Licoricia, or a member of her family, later acquired the Jewry Street house and regained possession of the synagogue. By 1290, the house and *scola* belonged to Licoricia's grandson, Jacob, son of Cokerel, and was valued at 16s. 6d.[112]

The *mikveh*

Another essential feature of Jewish religious practice was the *mikveh* (ritual bath), which was filled from a fresh flowing source of water. Women immersed themselves in the *mikveh* after giving birth and every month a week after menstruation ended. It was also used by both men and women to purify themselves before Jewish holy days and on a range of other ritual occasions, as well as for the purification of cooking and eating utensils. The location of the Winchester *mikveh* is not known, but there certainly

A *mikveh* from the City of London's medieval Jewish quarter, discovered in 2001. Mid 13th century.

would have been one, and it would probably have been situated as close to the synagogue as possible. Two medieval *mikveot* have been discovered in London, on Catte Street (now Gresham Street) and Milk Street, both close to the synagogues.

Remains of medieval *mikveot* have survived in many parts of Europe. A *mikveh* in Cologne dates from as early as the ninth century. Some of these were very impressive structures with long flights of steps leading to a large, vaulted chamber containing a stone pool or basin supplied by fresh water. Others, including in England, were on a more modest scale and were often in the cellar of a private house.[113] As with the location of synagogues, this was at least partly so the *mikveh* could be reached easily, safely and without attracting unwanted attention. Licoricia's house on Jewry Street had access to fresh water, an essential requirement for a *mikveh*, and it is possible that she built herself a private *mikveh* within the house, as her friend Benedict Crespin had done in London.[114]

The cemetery

Of equal if not more importance to the synagogue was the Jewish cemetery, which in medieval Winchester lay outside the city walls on the hill to the west of the city, immediately behind the castle's western moat. The location met the king's dictat that Jewish cemeteries must be outside the Christian city boundaries, and also satisfied Jewish rules that burial grounds must be more than fifty cubits from the homes of the living. Jews called their cemetery the *Bet Olam* (House of Eternity) or *Bet Chayim* (House of Life), while Christians referred to it euphemistically as the *hortus iudeorum*, or Jews' Garden.

The Jewish cemetery in Winchester occupied a large plot of land, rented by the Jews from the Priory of St Swithun's.[115] For well over a hundred years, from 1177 until the mass expulsion of 1290, this was the final resting place not only for the Jews of Winchester but for many neighbouring Jewish communities in the south of England. Licoricia was almost certainly buried here after her death in 1277. Her bones in all likelihood lie here still.

A key consideration for the location of the cemetery was access to fresh running water. According to Jewish law, the body of the deceased must be washed in a continuous flow of water before burial in a room or building used only for this purpose called the *Bet Tohorah* (House of Purification). Those who carried out this essential and solemn task were required to purify their hands in fresh flowing water before and after doing so. Precise customs varied from one community to another, but preparing the corpse for burial was considered the highest form of charity in Judaism, since the recipient was not able to express their gratitude.[116] The location of the *Bet Tohorah* in Winchester has not been identified but, in 1974–75 and 1995, part of the medieval cemetery was uncovered during excavations on the corner of what is now Crowder Terrace and Mews Lane. Crowder Terrace may derive its name from the Anglo-Norman word *crude* or *crute* (also linked to the word *grotto* in Italian), meaning an underground vault or crypt. The Jewish cemetery may have been located here because it was near a building with an underground chamber containing a spring or well for washing and preparing the dead for burial.[117]

Another possibility for the *Bet Tohorah* is a property on Wodestrete, now Romsey Road, which ran close to the cemetery's northern boundary. This property belonged to Licoricia's son Benedict and its location would have provided the Jewish community with direct access to the cemetery. After the 1290 expulsion, when Jewish belongings were sold off, the record of items in the property include reference to 'a stone on which the Jews washed bodies prior to burial'[118], suggesting that Benedict's Wodestrete property may have functioned as the cemetery's House of Purification.

The fair, the castle and the gaol

While Licoricia and her co-religionists had their own separate and distinct religious and social realms and were largely left to manage their own internal affairs, they were also part of the warp and weft of everyday life in medieval Winchester. They walked the same streets, came and went from the city by the same gates, plied their trades alongside their neighbours and bought and sold food and other produce at the same fairs and markets.

St Giles Fair, held each year at the end of August on St Giles Hill to the east of the city, was a big draw for both Jews and Christians. Established by William II in 1096, the fair was initially a three-day event but had expanded

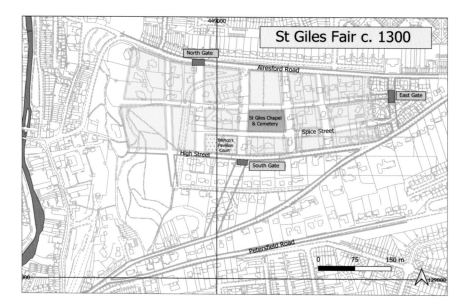

St Giles Fair c. 1300

A plan of St Giles Fair, Winchester in 1300. The medieval city and the river Itchen are down the hill to the left of the illustration.

by the middle of the twelfth century into a sixteen-day extravaganza that was still flourishing in Licoricia's day. Every year a whole pop-up town sprang to life on St Giles Hill, with trading booths, walkways, and places to eat, drink and sleep. A major centre for Anglo-French trade, the fair also attracted merchants from all over Europe. Traders from France, Spain and Italy were regular figures at the fair, as well as many Jewish traders and moneylenders from England and abroad. The scale and prestige of the fair in turn reflected the power of Winchester's bishops, for whom it generated a great deal of income.[119]

Winchester Jews also attended open court sessions, public meetings and tribunals, which in Licoricia's day took place in the magnificent Great Hall of the castle, built by Henry III between 1222 and 1236 and probably funded in part by Jewish taxes.[120] Licoricia seems to have enjoyed particularly cordial relations with the king and regularly attended the castle when he was resident. As a leading local and regional moneylender, she would have been a familiar face at legal hearings in the Great Hall.

The castle played a double-edged role for the Jews as both a place of refuge in times of trouble and as a prison. When tallages or large fines were due, leading members of the community were often held hostage in the castle prison until the sums were paid. In 1287, during the terrible final years for England's medieval Jewry, the entire community was taken hostage to force them to pay the tallage demanded by Edward I. Before the construction of the Jews' Tower in the 1240s, the medieval county gaol on Jewry Street (now the site of a pub) served the same double purpose. Licoricia's first husband, Abraham of Kent, was imprisoned there in 1225, as was Abraham Pinche in 1235.

Wealth and health

By the time Licoricia and Abraham settled in the city, probably in the early 1220s, Winchester was the third wealthiest Jewry in England, after London and York.[121] It had fallen to tenth place by 1241, but over the next decade its fortunes recovered and by 1255 it was equal to Lincoln as the most prosperous Jewry outside of London, in large part thanks to the personal wealth of Licoricia and her son Benedict.

Winchester's Jewry may have been one of the most important in England but, in terms of actual people, none of the Jewries were very big. At its peak in the early thirteenth century, the Winchester Jewry probably numbered between 150 and 300 people out of an overall population of around 3,000. (Winchester's total population had shrunk by then from around 13,000 at its peak in the early twelfth century.)[122] Its size fluctuated greatly during the thirteenth century, enlarged at times by Jews forced out of other towns, and depleted at other times when life for Jews in Winchester became too unsafe and they themselves relocated.

Health and wealth were closely connected, then as now. Licoricia herself would seem to have enjoyed both, but the majority of Winchester's Jews most likely did not. Analysis of skeletons excavated from the Jewish cemetery found that many of the children had rickets (as did many Christian children), a strong indicator of poverty.[123] In general, however, infant mortality and anaemia were lower amongst Jewish children in England, and Jewish families were larger. Jewish women also seem to have lived longer than their Christian counterparts.[124] These differences may reflect a greater degree of communal care for the poor and vulnerable, an ethical duty

A near-complete miniature jar, late 11th or 12th century. Excavated at St Aldate's, Oxford in 2016, the medieval Jewish quarter, by Oxford Archaeology. The jar showed that the Jewish community kept kosher.

in Judaism.[125] They also suggest better hygiene, medical skills and nutrition amongst Jewish communities.

Better health may have been an unintended benefit of Jewish dietary laws, which forbade Jews from eating shellfish and certain kinds of meat and fish, including pork, eel and oysters, all popular with the general population in medieval England. It was also forbidden for Jews to mix meat and dairy in the same meal, cook them in the same utensils or eat them from the same plates. Meat, as already mentioned, had to come from animals slaughtered in the prescribed manner (*shechita* in Hebrew). A combination of these restrictions led to a higher reliance on poultry, fish and vegetables in the Jewish diet. Analysis of animal bones and pottery fragments excavated in 2016 from part of the medieval Jewish quarter in Oxford found abundant evidence of poultry and a total absence of any forbidden foods.[126] Three-quarters of the bones were goose and chicken, which was extremely unusual for the medieval population overall. Organic residue analysis of fats extracted from the pottery fragments also revealed that meat and dairy were never cooked in the same pots. This provides clear evidence for the first time that the rules of *kashrut* were observed by Jews in medieval England.

Appearance and culture

In their external appearance, Jews in medieval Winchester were probably indistinguishable from Christians. (The main reason why Jews were required to identify themselves with the *tabula* and *pileum* was to make them more obviously different from Christians). Jewish women, as far as we know, wore their hair and dressed in the fashions typical of the day.[127] Records of wealthier medieval Jewish women's belongings include 'robes of bluet, shawls from Rouen, a cape of perse with silver and gold tassels, tunics and supertunics of shot silk trimmed with rabbit fur, a tunic dyed blood red and trimmed with squirrel fur'.[128]

What distinguished the Jews, besides their religion and religious customs, was their Norman origins and continuing close connections with their co-religionists in France. Until the early thirteenth century, Jews in England and Normandy were a single community straddling the Channel, rather than two distinct communities. The everyday language of Jews living in England was Norman-French (although they also spoke and wrote Hebrew and probably knew at least some Anglo-Saxon English). In addition to their Hebrew names, many English Jews also had French names, such as Deuledone, Bonamie and Belaset. They regularly traded with French merchants and imported food, clothing and kosher wine from France. There are also records of English Jews paying for permission to return to Rouen or illegally fleeing to France in times of trouble. In 1265, during a period of violent attacks, some Jewish families sent their children and nurses to France for safety.

The English *Bet Din* (court of Jewish law) was in charge of the English Jewry's internal affairs but remained in close contact with the Paris *Bet Din*, and many English Jews had family members living across the Channel. Rabbi Joseph of Colchester, for

Passover preparations. A sheep being slaughtered and a ram being skinned. Early 14th century manuscript, Catalonia, Spain example, was the son of Rabbi Yehiel, a leading Talmudic scholar and head of the Paris *yeshiva*. In the 1250s Joseph commissioned a magnificent bronze cauldron, known as the Bodleian Bowl (now in the Ashmolean Museum in Oxford); its decorative features include the French fleur-de-lys. It was given to the Colchester Jewish community in around 1260, probably in return for helping to fund the journey made soon after by Joseph and his father to the Holy Land.[129]

Yet even these close links with France would not have marked out the Jews of Winchester as especially unusual. There were many Normans living in the city, French names were commonplace and the language of the court was Anglo-Norman. English was the mother tongue of the peasantry, but French and Latin were essential for social and political advancement. This

The Bodleian Bowl, a two handled tripod cauldron, cast with a Hebrew inscription in relief about its girth. Given to the Jews of Colchester about 1260. In the seventeenth century, it was found in a disused moat in Norfolk, perhaps with a hoard of money inside it.

reflected the European-wide cultural dominance of France (and French) in the Middle Ages.[130] The bishop himself was French, as was the queen, Eleanor of Provence and, by descent, the king, not to mention many other members of the royal family and entourage. The French nobility may well have appreciated the cultural familiarity and relative sophistication and education of the Anglo-Norman Jews with whom they came into contact.

An integrated community

Throughout their time in Winchester, despite making up less than 10 per cent of Winchester's population, the Jews made an active economic contribution to the city and some at times were participating at the highest levels of local government, including and most notably Licoricia and later her son Benedict. These connections with the ruling elite were enabled and valued by some of Winchester's Christian citizens, deeply resented by others. As a community, their fluctuating fortunes were enmeshed in the wider context of the city's economic and political fortunes, and the way they were treated, individually and as a group, was likewise intimately connected to the governance of Winchester and to the city's wider role in the country as a whole.

The Jewry in turn changed and adapted: from the mid-century to the late thirteenth century it formed 'a multi-layered and fast-evolving community', straddling the breadth of Winchester society, from the secular and mercantile to the political and religious.[131] While the Jews of Winchester were a small community in terms of numbers, they were neither socially segregated nor geographically isolated. Like Jews in other parts of England, they remained closely connected with their co-religionists in England and Normandy, as well as in other parts of France and the Rhinelands, and through their activities in trade, finance, law and scholarship they came into contact with Jews and non-Jews in and far beyond the bounds of Winchester.

4

A WOMAN OF WORTH
The Life of Licoricia

Licoricia probably arrived in Winchester as a young and recently married woman sometime between 1215 and 1220. As a Jew she was part of a small minority group, but as an inhabitant of medieval Winchester, a royal city and the cathedral seat of one of country's richest bishops, she was now situated at the heart of Anglo-Norman England. Winchester was always much more than a backdrop to Licoricia's story. She spent around fifty years living in the city, moved in the highest circles of its society and was directly affected by its periods of both prosperity and turbulence.

Almost nothing is known of Licoricia's parentage or childhood but her father may have been Lumbard of Winchester, suggesting she might have grown up in the city. In financial records, however, she is sometimes referred to as Licoricia of Canterbury, which at the start of the thirteenth century was the second wealthiest Jewry in the country.[132] Her first husband, Abraham of Kent, had business dealings in Canterbury, making it likely this is where they both came from.[133] Abraham was also known as 'of Winchester', indicating he had business interests there too.

Jewish women in medieval England married early, often as young as eleven or twelve years of age.[134] The same was true of many Christian women at this time. Eleanor of Provence was twelve years old when she married twenty-eight-year-old Henry III in 1236. The first of their five children, Edward, was born three years later. Henry's sister, Eleanor, was betrothed at the age of six and married at the age of ten (although the marriage would not have been consummated until she was older). Wherever

(Left) **Licoricia meeting King Henry III in the Great Hall, Winchester**

Licoricia's birth family came from, she would have moved to be with her husband after they married. Over the next few years, the couple had three sons, Isaac (also known as Cokerel), Benedict (also known as Baruch) and Lumbard, and a daughter named Belia. By the early 1220s, if not before, the family had settled in Winchester.[135]

In 1225 disaster struck. Abraham, along with five other Winchester Jews, was accused of the murder of a Christian child.[136] Abraham and two of the other accused were found guilty by the highly imperfect justice system and their chattels (everything they owned) were confiscated. The usual punishment for murder was hanging, but there is no record of Abraham being hanged. In fact, for the next nine years there is no mention of him at all.

In 1234 Licoricia appears for the first time in the official records, described in Latin as 'Licoricia, who *was* the wife of Abraham of Kent', making it clear that she was by then a widow.[137] Newly, or not-so-newly bereaved, she was still living in Winchester with her four children and, as the records also reveal, she was by now making substantial business transactions in her own right.

Those nine silent years between 1225 and 1234 are tantalising. How did Licoricia and her children survive financially after Abraham's chattels were confiscated? How was she affected by his murder conviction and death, whether by execution or some other cause? Did she have access to money of her own? How and when did she launch her independent business activities? And where did she learn the necessary financial skills to become so successful so quickly?

Answers to many of these questions remain unanswered and unanswerable. Surviving sources, for example legal documents, were often negatively biased towards the Jews. Much else went unrecorded or was later lost or destroyed. As a result, piecing together the precise details of Licoricia's life is not straightforward, but other historical evidence about medieval Winchester and the Anglo-Jewry go some way to building a picture of the day-to-day world in which she lived and some of the people with whom she associated. What is clear from the surviving sources is that over the course of the next thirty years she successfully consolidated and expanded her wealth and influence through a combination of astute financial invest-

The Great Hall, Winchester Castle, where Licoricia met King Henry III

ment, effective management of her assets, canny collaborations with other financiers and a brief but superbly strategic second marriage.

The earliest documented evidence of Licoricia's business activities dates from January 1234, when 'Peytavin and Lycorez, Jews of Winchester' were ordered to let a certain Hugh Sanzaver off paying the interest on the £10 they had lent him, a sum large enough at that time to buy a brand-new, fully fitted ship.[138] A second mention of Licoricia in the same year records that William of Hamtun (Hampshire) owed her 10 marks, which he was ordered to repay at the rate of 2 marks a year.[139] These records reveal that she was making loans in partnership with other Jews as well as by herself.

It was not unusual by the mid-thirteenth century for medieval Jewish women to be moneylenders, both independently and jointly with their husbands or other family members.[140] A Winchester example of a mother and son business partnership is a woman called Glorietta and her son Samkin. A number of Jewish women seem to have been actively involved in the business of their husband, and there are also many examples of

Jewish women forming partnerships with each other. References to Jewish women moneylenders are ubiquitous in administrative records from the thirteenth century, 'particularly in the surviving and published plea rolls of the Exchequer of the Jews'.[141]

One of the most successful female Jewish financiers in the generation before Licoricia was Chera of Winchester.[142] Chera was head of a hugely successful family consortium, which included her four sons (amongst them Abraham Pinche, master of the Winchester *scola*), several daughters and at least three step-sons. In 1206, Chera loaned £20 to Hyde Abbey in Winchester. In the 1210 Bristol tallage, which demanded the enormous sum, reportedly, of 60,000 marks and was still being collected in 1211, Chera's consortium had to pay over £1,000, the largest sum of any one family in the country that year.[143] When they were unable to raise the required amount, Chera and her second husband, Isaac the Chirographer, were held hostage in Bristol and Winchester respectively. They were still in prison at the time of violent attacks on the Jewries of both cities in 1215, when many Jews were murdered. Being in prison probably helped save their lives. They were finally released on the death of King John in 1216.

When Chera married Isaac the Chirographer in 1210, he was a wealthy widower and had been living in Winchester for nearly twenty years. The couple worked together as business partners and also acted at times as agents for the Jewish magnate, Isaac of Norwich. After her husband's death in around 1218, Chera took over the moneylending business, making loans to 'Jew and Christian alike, in Hampshire and out of it'.[144]

Chera seems to have got on very well with her step-son Benedict Crespin (son of her first husband), who was a successful attorney and often represented his step-mother in court. She also worked closely with her eldest son Abraham Pinche and, together with her other sons and Benedict Crespin, the family had frequent and profitable dealings with the bishop, enabling him to secure land and greatly expand his wealth and power. When Chera died in 1221, her children inherited a flourishing business. Later that year, they had to pay 50 per cent of the total Jewish tallage for Winchester.

Two of Chera's sons, Deulebene and Elias, worked in partnership with Licoricia at times, as did her daughter-in-law, Belia (wife of Deulebene). Belia was a close friend of Licoricia and the two women may even have been related in some way, because several of their children and grand-children had the same names, suggesting they may have had ancestors in common.[145] Their grandsons later would also work together.

The years 1232 to 1236 were extremely difficult for Belia. Her husband Deulebene, master of the Winchester *scola*, died, and his brother Abraham Pinche took over the role. Pinche had been one of the co-accused with Licoricia's husband in 1225, and in 1232 he was once more the victim of an accusation of ritual murder after a one-year-old boy was found strangled near St Swithun's Priory. Pinche was accused of buying the baby from its nurse to use it as a ritual sacrifice.[146] Lurid but unsubstantiated rumours circulated that the child's body had been mutilated and its eyes and heart plucked out. Public feeling was running so high against the Jews that the entire Jewry was locked up temporarily for its own protection.

The child's mother was eventually found guilty of the murder and Pinche's name was officially cleared, but worse was to come. Three years later, in 1235, only a few months after taking over as *scola* master, the unfortunate and evidently deeply unpopular Pinche was arrested yet again, this time on historic charges of theft.[147] In February the following year Pinche was found guilty and sentenced to death. His punishment was severe even by the harsh standards of the day. Dragged through the city tied to a cart, he was then hanged on the gallows in front of the gaol. Most unusually, his corpse was denied burial in the Jewish cemetery and was instead buried at the foot of the gallows, which stood directly opposite his Jewry Street house.

In Winchester's small and close-knit Jewish community, the death of Deulebene and executions of Abraham and Pinche would have deeply affected the Jewry, Licoricia included, for these men and their families were her friends, neighbours, colleagues, and co-religionists. On top of personal grief, there were also pressing money issues to attend to. Licoricia had no inheritance fees to pay as her late husband's chattels had already been confiscated, but after Deulebene died, Belia was faced with finding the huge sum of 600 marks to be able to keep two-thirds of his bonds.[148]

By the end of the decade, however, despite the challenges of widowhood, or perhaps because of them, both Licoricia and Belia had established themselves as important moneylenders on the Winchester scene. In

1239 Licoricia, Belia and one of Chera's daughters, Blanche, all paid sums in the Winchester tallage, a measure of their success as financiers.

In around 1245, Belia remarried and moved to Bedford with her second husband, Pictavin, son of Benedict, a successful moneylender and the Bedford chirographer. He and Belia had two more sons, Jacob and Benedict, and the family lived in the Parish of St Paul's. Two sons from her first marriage, Moses and Lumbard, stayed on in Winchester to take care of her business interests there. Despite now living several hundred miles apart, Belia and Licoricia stayed in touch. They were still in contact more than two decades later, in 1258, when Belia sent Licoricia a precious gold ring to give to the king as a gift. The ring was somehow mislaid and a neighbour called Ivetta accused Licoricia of stealing it. While the accusation was being investigated, Licoricia was imprisoned in the Tower of London, until the real thief was discovered to have been none other than Ivetta.

Being a widow was not an impediment to Licoricia's career as a financier. Compared to other women in medieval England, widowed Jewish businesswomen enjoyed a high level of freedom and protection. Wives who had previously been invisible business partners were able to become active in their own right after their husbands died.[149] They could set up and head family firms, and they were also free to work independently, which seems to have been Licoricia's preference. The *ketubah* (Jewish marriage contract) often ring-fenced money for the bride that was only to be released if she were widowed. Licoricia herself may have benefited from such an arrangement, which could explain how she recovered financially after her first husband's death.[150]

Widowhood also created other kinds of opportunities. If a widow had inherited considerable wealth from a previous marriage, as both Chera and Belia had, she was now in a good position to make a strategic new marriage, and this was certainly one way for a woman to advance socially and financially. It was also, of course, a way to hold on to income and assets after a spouse died. The king, who always kept a close eye on his Jewish property, took a keen interest in remarriages between wealthy Jewish couples, and on at least one occasion demanded payment in return for granting permission to remarry.

David of Oxford

Licoricia was independently wealthy by 1240, but the events of the next four years of her life radically transformed her situation, catapulting her up the financial ranking to become one of the wealthiest Jews in England and the country's richest Jewish woman. The vehicle for this transformation was her second marriage to David of Oxford.

David and Licoricia probably first met in Winchester, where he had business interests and business partners, among them Chera's step-son Benedict Crespin.[151] By the time they decided to marry, David was in his fifties or sixties while Licoricia was probably in her mid to late thirties. As a wealthy young widow with local influence, high-ranking connections and a firm head for business, Licoricia would have been quite a catch. The personal qualities she must surely have possessed to gain the attention and favour of the king can only have added to her allure. David, furthermore, was in need of an heir and, unlike his own wife, Muriel, who after many years of marriage was still childless, Licoricia had already produced at least four healthy children. David's appeal was even easier to understand: he was one of the six richest Jews in England, a man endowed with great wealth, power and status in the Jewish community. If Licoricia was a catch, so for sure was David.

Here then were the makings of a medieval Jewish power couple, hindered only by the not insignificant problem that David was already married. Divorce in medieval England was extremely unusual, and for Christians permission to divorce was difficult to obtain. Amongst Jews it was also frowned upon. It was also a serious matter, although Judaism did not ban divorce on religious grounds and consensual divorce was permitted. According to Talmudic law, a wife could be divorced without her consent, but unless she had committed a major offence the husband would have to pay back the full amount of the *ketubah* (the original marriage settlement), which acted as an effective deterrent in most cases. However, one of the four decrees attributed to the leading medieval Talmudist Rabbeinu Gershom (c. 960–1040) was that (contrary to Talmudic law) a woman might not be divorced without her consent. By the thirteenth century, this had become the established custom among Ashkenazi Jews.

David of Oxford's house, Oxford. David lived in Oxford from about 1216 to 1244. Drawing by Wendy Bramall, 2015

Notwithstanding these impediments, in 1242 David succeeded in persuading the English *Bet Din* to grant him a divorce from Muriel, possibly on the grounds of their lack of children. But Muriel was determined not to be cast aside without a fight. She immediately began to contest the decision, rallying influential family members and friends to support a petition to the Paris *Bet Din* to overturn the divorce, which after due deliberation it did.

Undeterred, David launched a rapid counter-attack, appealing to Henry III for help. This was a bold and shrewd move on David's part. The king was never going to look kindly on being told what *his* Jews could or could not do by a foreign authority, and a non-Christian one at that. Nor was Henry going to risk losing access to David's considerable wealth. Henry would have known (or quickly have been made aware) that if David disobeyed the ruling of the Paris *Bet Din*, it would be entitled to confiscate his property.

David's direct appeal to Henry meant that he and Licoricia now had the king's political and financial self-interests on their side. The king promptly issued two letters that decided the matter. The first letter was addressed to the leading members of the English *Bet Din*, threatening them with 'grave punishment' if they interfered in any way with David's wish to divorce or remarry.[152] The second letter, dated 27 August 1242, banned any further tribunals concerning the Jews of England. Muriel and her supporters were ordered to appear before the king's acting regent, Walter de Grey, the

Archbishop of York, to justify their illegal appeal to the Paris *Bet Din*. The letter ended by stipulating that 'David of Oxford [shall not] be coerced by the Jews to take or hold any woman to wife except of his own free will'.[153] In short, David had won.

A love match, a strategic alliance, or a mixture of the two? Whatever the answer, Licoricia and David were both determined and confident personalities, and additionally empowered by their individual and combined wealth and influence and their close connections with the king. With royal permission to do as they pleased, the couple married without further delay and Licoricia moved to Oxford to live with her new husband in his imposing stone mansion on Fish Street (modern-day St Aldate's), right in the heart of medieval Oxford. This house survived until 1771 and is now the site of the modern town hall. The vaulted stone ceilings of one of the cellars of the original medieval Jewish properties that once stood there can still be seen to this day.

The following year, Licoricia gave birth to the longed-for son and heir, whom the couple named Asher, meaning 'happy' or 'blessed', although he was also known by the pet name of Douceman or Sweetman.[154] Things were rather less happy for poor Muriel, who had meanwhile moved into a smaller house on St Edward's Street, which also belonged to David and was in uncomfortably close proximity to his main property on Fish Street, where he was now living with his new wife and

Ring from the Erfurt hoard, Germany, probably hidden during the Black Death pogroms, 1349. This was a ceremonial ring used in wedding ceremonies.

son. St Edward's Street was demolished when Christ Church was built and is today part of Blue Boar Quad.

Licoricia was now First Lady of one of England's oldest and most securely established Jewries. Like Winchester, Oxford was a city with a strong royal presence, a castle and a mint. The Jewry numbered around 120 to 200 people and played an active role in the city as, amongst other occupations, scribes, landlords, moneylenders and pawnbrokers. Only a few years earlier, in 1240, Robert Grosseteste (the Chancellor of Oxford University and Bishop of Lincoln) had banned students from taking out any kind of loan from Jewish moneylenders after the libraries had been stripped of books held in pawn and the level of student debts had led to rioting.

One of Licoricia's neighbours was Jacob of Oxford, a leading Jewish magnate, who lived in a mansion on Fish Street, almost directly opposite her new home. She would have known Jacob for another reason too: his father, the great scholar Master Moses, was one of the members of the English *Bet Din*, which had granted David his divorce from Muriel. A major property owner, Jacob at one point owned or had an interest in 10 per cent of all the properties in Oxford. In the 1260s, Jacob sold two tenements on St John Street (now Merton Street) to Walter de Merton, which became part of the newly founded Merton College.[155] He also designed, built and sold to de Merton the first purpose-built residential academic hall on a nearby site on Pennyfarthing Street (now Pembroke Street).

David was born and raised in Lincoln, but by 1216 he had moved to Oxford and changed his toponym from 'of Lincoln' to 'of Oxford'. He was already very successful by this time, with business activities spanning at least seven counties. His myriad clients ranged from local landowners to senior clergy, high-ranking noblemen and members of the royal family. He acted as a financier to the king, and to the king's sister Eleanor de Montfort, Countess of Leicester. In 1239, along with two other leading Jewish magnates, Aaron and Leo of York, David had been tasked with raising money from the Jewry to fund a Crusade for the king's brother, Richard Earl of Cornwall. Four years later, in 1241, a further tallage of 20,000 marks was imposed, a substantial proportion of which came from these same three men.

David also used his considerable influence to help the country's Jewish community, securing properties for synagogues in Worcester and Oxford,

Deed of sale of Jacob of Oxford to Walter de Merton, royal chancellor, relating to the sale of houses for the 'Scholars and Brethren of the House of Scholars', 1267

and representing the Jews at court, where he did his best to protect their interests and keep tallage demands as low as possible.

As well as paying vast sums in local taxes and other one-off payments, David kept on the right side of the king with regular personal gifts of cash and fine horses and, on one occasion, an annual pair of new gold spurs. David, for his own part, seems to have thoroughly enjoyed the fruits of his financial success. Besides owning one of the grandest houses in Oxford, he kept a stable of palfreys (expensive horses designed for riding rather than hard labour) and amassed in his lifetime an impressive personal library of precious Hebrew books.

Wealth gave the major Jewish financiers like David a degree of bargaining power, but it could never be relied upon, and David's reputation for driving a hard bargain must therefore be seen in the context of the times. Moneylending was a risky business and Jewish loans were always insecure. Hefty tallages or fines could wipe out individual fortunes at a stroke; debts were often reduced or cancelled by the king at no notice, and records of loans were not infrequently disputed, not paid, or destroyed by the debtors themselves.

Between 1230 and 1240, the king pardoned or suspended thirty of David's debts. A further debt of £110 owed to David by Simon de Montfort was pardoned in 1244, even though David had earlier made significant loans to de Montfort's wife Eleanor.[156] From the Jewish financiers' point of view, taking a tough stance on enforcing payments, setting interest rates as high as possible, and taking property and possessions as security on loans were all necessary ways to protect their inevitably precarious investments.

In 1241 Henry III had called a parliament of the Jews, threatening the sheriffs of Nottingham, Cambridge, Lincoln, York, Bedford, Norfolk and Suffolk with dire consequences if they failed to make sure the Jewish representatives attended:

> The King to the sheriff of Northamptonshire, greetings. We command you, as you love yourselves and all yours and so that we do not most grievously seize upon you by force, that you cause to come before us at Worcester on the Sunday next before Ash Wednesday six of the wealthier and more powerful Jews of Northampton, and from each town in your shire in which Jews dwell one or two Jews according to their numbers, to treat with us of their utility as of ours, knowing that unless these Jews come at the aforesaid time, we will so aggrieve you in consequence by your body and by your chattels that you will forever feel our hand to grieve you immoderately.[157]

The Jewish 'parliament' met in Worcester soon after, with twenty-one Jewries represented by 109 Jews. The official purpose of the meeting was to get the Jews to agree amongst themselves how to pay the upcoming tallage. In the process, the Worcester Parliament also exposed the huge disparities in wealth between the most prosperous Jews and the rest of the Jewish population. This issue was addressed by the Jewries' leaders and helped to ensure a more equitable and proportionate allocation of payments from then on.

Widowed again

In February 1244, just two years after their marriage, David suddenly died, leaving Licoricia with an infant son and facing potential financial catastrophe. In David's case, the inheritance tax (known as 'relief') due on his estate was an enormous sum, and the burden of raising it now fell solely on Licoricia. In medieval England when a Jew died, any heirs had to pay for the right to inherit. The value of all the deceased person's property was assessed and a sum equal to one-third of the value was then charged to their heirs. This sum could be paid in cash in agreed instalments, which enabled heirs to retain possession of all of the deceased person's assets, but if this sum could not be raised in cash, the heirs were obliged to hand over bonds and other debts equal to the value of the one-third due to the Crown, or face imprisonment. Turning bonds into cash was tedious and time-consuming, so straight cash payments were preferred whenever possible. If the king wished, he could simply keep the whole estate, as Henry II had done when Aaron of Lincoln died.

The exact value of David's very substantial wealth was not known when he died. On news of his death, all the *archae* across the country containing official records of his financial transactions were locked and the chests transferred to the Jewish Exchequer in London for assessment. David's many debtors immediately began contesting the amounts they owed, terrified the treasury might either demand full repayment of their loans, or worse, cancel the pledge to the deceased Jew and reassign it on harsher terms to someone else.

To prevent any attempt at interference from Licoricia, she was instantly taken hostage in the Tower of London, where she remained a prisoner for the next eight months, until the complicated process of calculating David's worth was completed. During her lengthy incarceration, Licoricia's own complex business interests were managed by six leading Jews, appointed to this task by the king. What happened to baby Asher while his mother was imprisoned in the Tower of London is not known. What is certain, however, is that delicate negotiations were going on behind the scenes to agree precisely how much Licoricia was going to have to pay to buy back the remainder of David's chattels, bonds and debts.

Eventually, a deal was struck. The price of repurchasing David's estate was set at 5,000 marks. Of this, 4,000 marks was earmarked for the building of a chapel at Westminster Abbey to house a lavish shrine to Edward the Confessor (1003–66), whom Henry III had made his patron saint.

The Tomb of Edward the Confessor, Westminster Abbey, London. Licoricia contributed the equivalent of millions of pounds today towards the building of the shrine as part of a deal with Henry III to secure the return to her of David's estate.

Licoricia was also ordered to pay an additional sum of £2,500 (around 1,700 marks) as a personal contribution to the new chapel. To get a sense of just how valuable David's estate must have been, compare the 5,000 marks Licoricia had to pay to the 400 marks Belia was obliged to raise when her first husband died in 1236, and the 735 marks when her second husband died in 1261. Both Belia's husbands were considered wealthy men.

The initial sums were enormous, but in return Licoricia was allowed to keep not just two-thirds of her late husband's debts and bonds, but all of them. Subject to the special order of the king, she was also exempted from any future tallages as long as she paid him the sum of 25 marks a year, a paltry amount in relation to her overall wealth.

How did Licoricia manage to strike such a favourable bargain? Perhaps it was in return for helping to finance the king's passion project of a shrine to his hero, Edward the Confessor. Or perhaps Henry calculated that relative leniency at this point was in his financial interest in view of the benefit to the Crown from her future business activities. Whatever the answer, Licoricia's future now appeared to be set fair. If her second marriage had greatly enhanced her position materially and socially, her second widowhood cemented both her wealth and her status. With her inheritance from David combined with her own assets, she was now the richest Jewish woman in medieval England.

An independent woman

Freed at last from the Tower of London, Licoricia and her son Asher returned to Winchester. From then until her death she lived in Jewry Street
in a large stone-built house with sufficient room for other members of
her family and household servants, a cellar where money and valuables
could be securely stored, and quite possibly the community *mikveh*. The
property came with an acre of land, which extended all the way back to
Fleshmonger Street, and probably included not only the Winchester *scola*,
but also a garden, orchard and space for domestic animals.[158]

With no children from David's first marriage, Licoricia also inherited all
of his properties in Oxford, apart from his main house on Fish Street, which
was seized by the Crown and used to maintain the *Domus Conversorum*,
a property in London to house Jewish converts to Christianity.[159] David's
mansion in Oxford was still standing well into the eighteenth century,
when it was torn down and eventually replaced by the current town hall.

Licoricia was probably in her early forties when David died in 1244 and
she was now in control of enough wealth to engage in substantial and
widespread business activities. As well as taking over David's business
interests, she forged new ones of her own, conducting much of this business from her home in Winchester. Amongst her Christian clients were
members of the aristocracy, the clergy and the royal family. When Henry
III was in Winchester, Licoricia was usually present at the castle, dealing
with the king's officials as well as with the king himself. She also made
loans to other Jews.

To be a successful lender at this level required more than just financial
acuity. A fair degree of interpersonal skill was also necessary to build rela-
tionships with clients, and careful judgement was called for when offering
advice or knowing when to agree to extend the terms of a loan, forgo part
of a debt or supply additional funding.[160]

For the next twenty or so years, as well as running her household and
domestic affairs, Licoricia regularly travelled around the country, managing her business interests, which by then extended over many counties. The journey from Winchester to London would have taken three to
four days, and from Winchester to York or Lincoln closer to two or three

weeks.[161] Money had to be transported physically in sacks and chests, and Licoricia would have made these journeys on horseback accompanied by armed guards to protect her and her money from attack and theft. The routes were carefully planned to ensure overnight stops were spent in towns with Jewries, where she could stay in safety. To limit the risks of carrying large sums of money from place to place, Licoricia also made use of local agents to collect payments in the various towns and cities where she had business interests.

Although Jewish women (like Christian women) were not meant to sign agreements or appear in court without a male attorney, there is plenty of evidence that some did, and Licoricia was one of them. Her name regularly appears in the plea rolls of the Exchequer of the Jews in relation to financial disputes. The most well-known of these disputes occurred in 1252 after the death of one of her clients, a cash-strapped Warwickshire landowner called Sir Thomas of Charlecote. Licoricia had inherited Sir Thomas's long list of debts from her husband David. One of these had been paid off not long after David's death in the form of a casket of jewels, but Sir Thomas was evidently still in financial difficulties, because in 1246 he had come to an arrangement with Licoricia to bundle all the remaining debts into a single loan, which he pledged to repay with interest over a period of six years. The total amount was £400 and the security on the loan was his estate, rent and chattels.

Two years later the situation became more complicated when Sir Thomas was found drowned in a lake on his estate, possibly murdered, although this was never proven. Had the creditor been a Christian, he would have been entitled to take possession of the estate and sell it. But different rules applied to Jewish creditors, who were only allowed to receive income from the estate for a year and a day, after which they had no further claim on it. Licoricia, however, continued to manage the estate and receive income from it for the next four years, and her activities may have included the selling of livestock, timber and possessions from tenements and farm buildings.[162] In doing so, she was in breach of the terms of the pledge and of the law, but she had good reason to think she could do as she pleased since she was acting with the explicit support of the king.[163]

In 1252, the infuriated heir of Sir Thomas, who had now come of age, took Licoricia to court. Undaunted, Licoricia counter-accused Sir

Thomas's son of having arranged his father's death to get out of paying the full debt owed to her. When the Hampshire court found in the son's favour, the king promptly overruled the court's decision, restored the estate to Licoricia and ordered a new trial, this time in London. Licoricia was held in the Tower of London while the trial was conducted, but even in prison she continued to receive income from the estate, thanks again to the king's intervention. Although Henry had attempted to stack the judges for the new hearing, the trial once more found Licoricia guilty as charged. Before the penalty was decided, however, the king interceded to limit her fine to the trifling amount of half a silver mark.

The Charlecote case reveals how valuable major Jewish moneylenders such as Licoricia were to the king, and how far he would go to protect them when his own financial interests were at stake, even when his interventions went against the law of the land. Royal preferential treatment of this kind did not make the king popular and would hardly have endeared Licoricia to her Christian debtors, but it may indirectly have assisted the Jewish community in Winchester, which at times seem to have been treated with particular leniency by Henry. In 1261, for example, the king ordered that his Winchester Jews should not be taxed too heavily. It is not impossible that Licoricia on occasion used personal influence to intercede on the Winchester Jewry's behalf.

Licoricia's success as a businesswoman after 1244 was all the more impressive because these were extremely difficult years for the Jewish community as a whole. The Worcester Parliament of 1241 had not only decided the tallage allocation, but also provided Henry III with a detailed picture of the Jews' individual and collective wealth.[164] For the next fifteen years, the king savagely plundered the Jewry for money, extracting three times the sums he had demanded in the previous two decades, heedless of the hardship this caused.[165] Between 1241 and 1256, the Jewry was forced to pay more than half of its total wealth in taxation, contributing around 10 per cent of the government's ordinary yearly revenues, despite being no more than 'one-tenth of one percent of the total English population'.[166] One consequence of the terrible difficulties endured by the English Jewry during these two decades was a sharp increase in the number of Jews driven to convert to Christianity to avoid starvation. As many as 10 per cent of the country's Jewish population appear to have taken this desperate route by the late 1250s.[167]

Even the most prosperous Jews were vulnerable. Aaron of York, one of the wealthiest Jewish magnates in 1241, had been bankrupted by 1255 as a result of the king's demands. The family of another leading Jewish magnate, Leo Episcopus of York, were likewise ruined in 1244 by the vast fine of 7,000 marks imposed on his heirs after his death. By 1252, the Jewry was on its knees. When the king made another huge tallage demand for 10,000 marks in 1254, Elias l'Eveske, then the head of the Jewry, pleaded with the king to let the Jews leave the country rather than continue to suffer from these crushing taxes. His pleas fell on deaf ears. It was in these years that Licoricia's deal with the king after David's death proved its value, since her exemption from paying tallages largely protected her from the devasting impact of these constant and punishing demands for money. But this would have been of no help to the rest of the Winchester Jewry, who now had to pay the city's assessment without Licoricia's help.

Licoricia and sons

The situation for Jews in general was becoming increasingly difficult by the 1250s. In 1253 the king issued the 'Statute Concerning the Jews', which imposed six of the repressive anti-Jewish measures from the 1222 Oxford Synod, and added seven more for good measure. The first of these decreed that no Jew remain in England unless he do the King service, and that from the hour of birth every Jew, whether male or female, serve Us in some way. Licoricia's own position was buffered by her personal wealth, and further protected by the fact that her three sons by her first husband were by this time grown men with financial enterprises of their own. All three worked with and helped their mother in various capacities.

Cokerel, her eldest, had two sons, Abraham and Jacob, and a daughter, whose name, like that of his wife, is not known. A financier and attorney, Cokerel acted in court cases for both Jews and Christians, and regularly represented his mother in her legal disputes.[168] Cokerel, whose name derives from his Hebrew name Isaac, meaning 'he laughs' (pronounced Yitzak or Yitzchok, hence Cok or Cokerel), lived in the grounds of Licoricia's property on Jewry Street until her death in 1277.

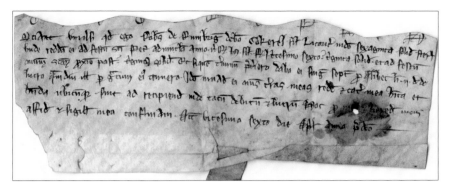

Bond by Robert de Rumbrige, to Cokerel son of Licoricia, 26 April 1252

Licoricia's regard for her firstborn son and her trust in his skills is evident from the fact that he was her right-hand man throughout the Charlecote case, and was in court on her behalf again in 1253 over a dispute about a loan to another landowner, Thomas Bigge. On the four occasions when Licoricia was in the Tower of London, in 1244, 1245, 1252 and the 1270s, she put Cokerel in charge of her loans, which he managed on top of numerous complex loans of his own. Several of his bonds have survived, one to Robert de Rumbrige in 1250 in which he is recorded as 'Cockerel fils Licorice, from Hampshire',[169] and the other in 1251 where he is recorded as 'Cockerell son of Licor the Jew'.[170]

In 1255, Cokerel himself was held hostage in the Tower, along with his brother Benedict, where they were taken while the Winchester Jewry was trying to meet the latest heavy tax demand, in this instance to enable the king to repay a loan from his brother Richard, Earl of Cornwall. As always, this method of raising cash for the Crown forced the Jews to call in loans at short notice and stoked hostility towards the Jewish moneylenders, through little fault of their own.

Lumbard, Licoricia's youngest son by Abraham, is first mentioned in the Exchequer Rolls in 1254, but he makes far fewer appearances in the official records than his older brothers. Lumbard had three sons of his own, called Cokerel, Solomon and Abraham. In 1273, he paid for permission to leave Winchester and move to Basingstoke. A few years later he moved again, this time to Devizes in Wiltshire, although he still had a house in

Winchester at the time of the 1290 expulsion. Lumbard was probably involved in moneylending to some extent, because in 1278, by which time conditions for the Jews in England were becoming ever more desperate, he was charged with exchange trespass (exchanging money at somewhere other than an official exchange) and ordered to hand over belongings worth the considerable sum of 40 marks.[171]

Far and away the most successful of Licoricia's children was her middle son, Benedict. An able and astute businessman, Benedict was a born risk-taker who resolutely tracked his way through the social and political power struggles that dominated the country during his adulthood. A prominent figure both locally and nationally, Benedict lived his whole life in Winchester, but his financial portfolio extended far beyond and many of his clients were from the highest levels of English society. He worked in parallel with his mother and occasionally in partnership with her and on several occasions acted as her attorney. He too was frequently involved in legal disputes related to his loans. In 1253, he brought an action against another Winchester Jew called Bonamy for the return of a Hebrew book worth 20 shillings. This was clearly an expensive volume and may have come to Benedict from David of Oxford's library when David died.

Benedict and his first wife Belassez had at least seven children: four sons and three daughters. In 1267 Benedict and Belassez were violently attacked by a mob led by the Prior of St Swithun's. The prior was subsequently ordered to pay Benedict £100 in compensation for personal injuries and damage to his property.[172] Belassez died not long after, possibly from injuries inflicted during the attack, and in 1273 Benedict married again. His second wife, Floria Le Blunde, was the extremely wealthy widow of one of his close friends and business partners, Solomon l'Eveske, another prominent financier. Like Licoricia's own second marriage, Benedict and Floria's match was financially strategic. With no children from her first marriage, Floria brought to her union with Benedict two-thirds of Solomon's estate, and when Floria died in 1275, Benedict was granted all her belongings as well as the loans of her first husband.

On top of his work as a moneylender, Benedict was a sought-after attorney, ran an import-export business in Southampton with his son Lumbard, and traded in wine, wool, salt and wheat. He owned numerous properties

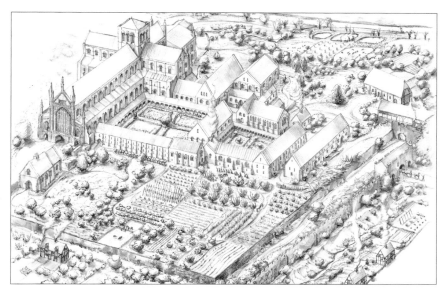

Reconstruction drawing depicting the Cathedral and Priory of St Swithun as it may have appeared at the time of the Dissolution, c. 1540. The Perpendicular window of the west end of the Cathedral postdates Licoricia

in both cities, as well as houses in York and Bristol. At the height of his success, Benedict was making the most of the 'strikingly close commercial relations between the Jews and the [wealthiest] citizens of Winchester',[173] and routinely socialising and doing business with Winchester's guildsmen, who ran the city. The mayor of Winchester, Simon le Draper, seems to have been a personal friend as well as one of Benedict's closest business associates.

It was Simon le Draper who, in 1268, was instrumental in getting Benedict elected as a member of the city's merchant guild, the first and only Jew in medieval England to be granted this privilege. His election on 5 May is recorded in the patent roll in words that were as warm as they were extraordinary:

> Know all men that I, Simon le Draper, Mayor of Winchester, with common counsel and assent of all bailiffs and citizens of the said city have received our beloved and faithful friend, Benedict fil Abraham, the Jew into full society of our liberty as a fellow citizen and fellow Guildsman.[174]

Benedict's election to the guild made him a full citizen of England, placing him on an equal footing with other members of the city's ruling council, and freeing him from many of the restrictions imposed on the Jews. For a start, he was no longer limited to owning property to live in himself or rent to other Jews, but could now purchase property outright for whatever purpose he pleased. Within just a few days of his election, he had bought several houses and shops in Winchester. As always, the ultimate beneficiary of Benedict's expanding wealth was the king, who may have privately authorised his election to the Guild.

While it may have pleased the king and Simon le Draper, Benedict's election went down very badly indeed with many of the ordinary towns-people of Winchester, who regarded his appointment as yet more evidence of the corruption of their ruling elite. The city promptly erupted in riots and there were violent attacks on the Jews and their property. The king eventually had to step in and set up a special group of guardians to protect the Jewry.

Criticisms of the city's ruling elite were probably not unfounded. Perks, backhanders and insider deals between guildsmen all helped grease the wheels of local power and it is likely that 'mutually advantageous if shady deals' were fairly commonplace.[175] Benedict himself was accused of sharp practice at times, but he was no different in this respect than the Christians he was doing business with. For the Jewish community, he was nevertheless an important representative. In the 1270s he served as the Jewish chirographer for Winchester and as escheator (the person in charge of supervising death duties and other fines) for the Jewry as a whole.

Licoricia's fourth and youngest son, Asher, her child by David of Oxford, seems to have been the closest to his mother and was quite possibly her favourite. Although he moved to Marlborough in Wiltshire in his twenties, he continued to work with Licoricia, acting as her financial agent in towns outside of Winchester. He appears to have moved back to Oxford at some point as a young man, living for a time in a house on what is now the High Street, as well as owning several other properties in the city. He was wealthy in his own right, thanks to his inheritance of valuable loans and properties from his father, to which he added loans of his own, and according to surviving records, he owned several properties in Winchester and Marlborough in addition to his Oxford property portfolio. His wife, Muriel, daughter of Samuel, was also a moneylender.

Asher was known as both 'son of Licoricia' and 'son of David', while Licoricia's older sons sometimes called themselves 'son of Licoricia', and sometimes 'son of Abraham' after their father. Only Cokerel used his mother's name throughout his life. Benedict was so successful he was also known as Benedict of Winchester.

It is hard to know whether there was anything significant in Lumbard and Benedict's less frequent use of Licoricia's name. Chera's children, by contrast, all used their mother's name and worked together as a family firm. Perhaps Lumbard and Benedict were less close personally to Licoricia, or it might have been

Detail of Asher, sculpture by Ian Rank-Broadley FRSS

useful for their own work to be seen as independent of their mother. The fact remains that when Licoricia had need of them throughout her life, all four of her sons provided practical support and professional skills to help her out.

Caught in the crossfire: The Second Barons' War

In 1263, Asher turned twenty. The whole country was simmering with political tension as the always delicate relationship between Henry III and his ambitious, arrogant and charismatic brother-in-law Simon de Montfort grew increasingly tense. De Montfort was the head of a confederation of rebellious barons who wanted more political power and autonomy and much tighter controls on the king's financial activities. A particular cause of resentment was royal trading in Jewish bonds.[176] The rebels also wanted to purge the country of 'aliens', as foreigners were known, while choosing to ignore the fact that de Montfort was French and therefore himself an alien.

A few years earlier de Montfort had led a revolutionary coup against Henry, which resulted in the king having to accept many of the rebel barons' demands, set out in the 1258 Provisions of Oxford. But Henry was not keen to be reduced to a puppet king and shilly-shallied on delivering and abiding by the radical changes he had promised. In 1261, the Pope agreed to absolve him of the oath he had made at Oxford, further enraging the barons. The situation was made more fraught still by long-running conflicts between the Church and the Crown, and many ordinary citizens, angry and restless for change, also supported the rebels. The result was civil war.

In 1264, after months of armed skirmishes, during which the opposing sides fought for control of key towns and ports, the armies of Simon de Montfort and King Henry met on the battlefield above the town of Lewes in Sussex. De Montfort had five hundred troops, Henry had three times that number, but despite the odds being against them, the rebels won the battle, declaring it a holy victory. Henry and his son Edward were captured and taken prisoner, and for a short period Simon de Montfort was the *de facto* ruler of England. He promptly cancelled nearly all Jewish loans, destroyed records of Jewish debts and banned moneylending by Jews. He reinstated moneylending the following year, however, having realised that he was missing out on a necessary source of income.

The Barons' War raged for over a year, but the rebels were finally defeated at the Battle of Evesham in 1265. Simon de Montfort and two of his sons, Henry and Guy, were deliberately mobbed and murdered in the course of the fighting. To drive home the royalist victory, de Montfort's body was castrated, decapitated and hacked to pieces by the king's men, before being triumphantly scattered across the battlefield. The dismembered body subsequently became a holy relic for de Montfort's supporters. Henry eventually resorted to digging up the body and throwing it away in an effort to quash his old rival's posthumous celebrity.

The war and its aftermath brought great suffering to the Jews, who were widely seen as agents of the king and complicit with his allies. Even before the war, mounting hostility towards the Jews had led to vicious assaults on many Jewries, during which Jewish homes were ransacked and many individual Jews lost their lives. In 1264 in the week running up to Palm Sunday, a supporter of de Montfort, called John Fitz John, led an attack on the London Jewry even more deadly than the attack on York in 1190. According to one chronicler:

> ... all the property of the Jews [was] carried off: as many [Jews] ... as were found being stripped naked, despoiled and afterwards murdered by night, to the number of more than 500. Those who survived were saved by the Justiciars and the Mayor, having been sent to the Tower before the slaughter took place.[177]

Simon de Montfort was not directly responsible for the London massacre, but he was certainly no friend of the Jews. His parents had played a significant role in massacres of Jews in southern France as part of their crusades against the Cathars, and in 1217 his mother, Alix de Montmorency, had forced the Jews of Toulouse to choose between conversion, expulsion or execution. One of Simon de Montfort's first acts on being made the 6th Earl of Leicester in 1230 had been to expel all the Jews from the lands he controlled, banishing them 'in my time or in the time of any of my heirs to the end of the world'. A zealous Christian with deep antipathy for the Jews, he was also influenced by the extreme anti-Jewish views of his spiritual mentor, Robert Grosseteste, who had died in 1253.[178]

From 1263 to 1267, the Jewries in Bristol, Canterbury, Gloucester, Lincoln, Cambridge, Bedford, Northampton, Norwich, Nottingham, Worcester and Winchester were targeted by violent mobs, whipped up by the political tensions, engrained antisemitic prejudice and resentment of Jewish moneylenders. In Lincoln, while the Jews themselves managed to flee to safety in time, the synagogue was burned to the ground. In Cambridge and Bedford, the *archae* were stolen and their contents destroyed. Destruction of the *archae* was devastating for Jewish moneylenders. The modern equivalent would be finding all your bank accounts had been emptied behind your back, along with proof that you had ever had a bank account or anything in it.

Winchester, too, suffered from violent conduct towards its Jewish community during and after the civil war. In June 1264, following attacks on the city's Jews by factions of local churchmen and their supporters, the king appointed twenty-four citizens to protect them. But this proved of little use the following year when de Montfort's son, Simon, on his way to help his father at Evesham, paused for three days in Winchester, where he and his men ransacked the city, looted the Jewry and destroyed the *archae* and all trace of many of the Jews' debts. Any Jews not safely locked in the castle were murdered in cold blood, or as the chronicler Robert of Gloucester put it: 'All the Jews of the town he slayed each one/ And wherever he found them, he left alive not one.' ('*All the gywes of the town he let slay echon/ That me in eni stede fonde he ne leude alive none.*')[179]

After the war Henry set about reasserting his authority, but the way he did so was a mixed blessing for the Jewish community. On the one hand, he seems to have been genuinely keen to rebuild the battered Jewry and took active steps to help the Jewish financiers get back on their feet by reinstating the debts that Simon de Montfort had cancelled and allowing the Jews to move to new towns. On the other hand, after confiscating rebel barons' lands as punishment, Henry then permitted them to buy back their estates but at vastly inflated rates, which frequently necessitated taking out loans from Jewish moneylenders. While this went some way to compensate the Jews for their lost bonds, it also led to more outbreaks of anti-Jewish violence. Following attacks on several Winchester Jews, Henry again intervened and in 1270 appointed a new set of guardians to protect them. But of the many individuals responsible for killing Jews during the 1260s, every single one was subsequently pardoned.

Licoricia was granted permission by the king to travel the country and search the *archae* in other towns for evidence of her lost loans, as were

Battle of Evesham and death of Simon de Montfort, 4 August 1265, from Chronica Roffense by Matthew Paris, 13th century

her sons Benedict, Isaac and Asher, and her old friend Belia. Belia had suffered greatly during the Barons' War. Her second husband, Pictavin, had died in around 1261, and she was working in partnership with her son Jacob by this time.[180] But repeated attacks on the Bedford Jewry from 1261 onwards put their lives and livelihoods in very real danger. At the height of the civil unrest, the Bedford *archa* was seized and all the chirographs recording Jewish loans were burned. Belia and her family also endured the trauma of her son Benedict being abducted and forcibly baptised by supporters of Simon de Montfort. Like many others, Belia's fortunes never really recovered.[181] In the 1270s, by which time she must have been in her sixties, she was imprisoned in the Tower of London for illegally selling a bond, probably to raise money for the still unpaid fine for inheriting her husband's loans after he died.[182]

Licoricia, too, was badly affected by the events of these years. She would have been considered old by the standards of the day and in 1270 she failed to turn up at a legal hearing, pleading she was 'too ill to stir'.[183] This may just have been a delaying tactic, but perhaps her health really was starting to fail by this time. Or perhaps the constant danger and difficulties of being an active moneylender no longer seemed worth the risks because from this time on she disappears from the public record. The last mention of her is in 1276, when the sheriffs of no fewer than seven different counties were 'ordered to produce the debts of Licorice'.[184]

Only Benedict emerged from the war relatively unscathed, possibly because his business interests were more diverse and geographically dispersed. With the royalists now back in charge, Benedict even managed to increase his wealth and standing in the next few years, thanks to his close connections with Simon le Draper, and many of Winchester's leading guildsmen and merchants. His controversial election to the guild took place just three years after the Battle of Evesham.

Edward I and Eleanor of Castile from Lincoln Cathedral

5

FROM MURDER TO EXPULSION

The Final Years of England's Medieval Jews

The last years of Licoricia's life were far from easy. The war was over, but conditions for the Jewry were becoming ever more precarious. As part of the ageing king's attempts to restore harmony with his barons and address their economic grievances, new statutes were passed that imposed severe restrictions on Jewish activities, social and financial. From 1253 Jews were banned from building synagogues, hiring Christian servants and paying fines to avoid having to wear the hated *tabula* badge. In 1269 Jews were banned from selling their bonds to Christians without royal permission, and banned from holding 'fee rents', which had previously enabled them to collect interest in perpetuity on debts owed by Christians. Fee rents were often negotiated in cases where the Christian debtor was unable to pay off a large loan. The attraction of a fee rent was that it was a life-time term, thus securing annual income for the Jewish moneylender and saving the debtor from having to sell off their land. But fee rents placed the Christian in a postion of 'perpetual servitude' to a Jew, which from a Christian theological perspective was considered a profound affront.[185] In 1271 the Jews were banned from renting property to Christians and, still worse, banned from owning the freehold in land or any kind of property, except the one they lived in. This left the Jews far more constrained in the kinds of financial transactions they could make and, in addition, with little way to protect their loans.

The situation deteriorated further after 1272 when Henry died and his son, Edward I, became king. A zealous Christian with deep antipathy for non-Christians, Edward was on Crusade with his wife, Eleanor of Castile, when he heard the news that his father had died. When they returned from Crusade in 1274, the new royal couple were crowned jointly in Westminster Abbey.

Throughout their long marriage, Edward and Eleanor were tenderly devoted to one another, but the royal couple were hard-hearted in equal measure in relation to the Jews. In 1273, the first year of his reign, Edward authorised a tax of one-third of all Jewish assets, the harshest tallage in over three decades, which led to the predictable hike in hostility towards the Jews. In Winchester, Simon le Draper was voted out of office as mayor in 1273 and replaced by his rival Roger de Dunstaple, known and popular for his strong anti-Jewish views. Roger de Dunstaple had been one of the 1270 guardians of the Jews, but in 1273 had switched his allegiances and not long after led a mob of thirteen men who violently assaulted Deudonne, the Winchester chirographer, ransacking and pillaging his house and valuables. Four years later, Licoricia's grandson Abraham (Benedict's son) was robbed and attacked so violently that his life was despaired of.

Perhaps in response to Dunstaple's election to mayor and the hostile environment he encouraged, many members of the Winchester Jewry left the city around this time, among them Licoricia's son Lumbard, who moved to Basingstoke in 1273. The following year, Lumbard's son Solomon also left the city and moved to Odiham. Another of Licoricia's grandsons, Aaron (son of Benedict), moved to Canterbury around the same time, where he was appointed the Jewish chirographer. He was joined there by his brother Cokerel and sister Belaset. The three siblings were still living in Canterbury in 1290.

Edward I was determined to get a grip of his financial problems, and one of the methods he fixed upon was to put an end to Jewish involvement in the country's cash flow. His influence had been central to the punitive statutes of 1269 and 1271, and now that he was king there was nothing to hold him back. Two years after his coronation, in a catastrophic development for the Jews, Edward issued the 1275 Statute of the Jewry. The Jews were henceforth completely banned from lending money at interest, whether on land or moveables, and interest accumulating on existing loans was frozen.[186] The statute also radically expanded the definition of

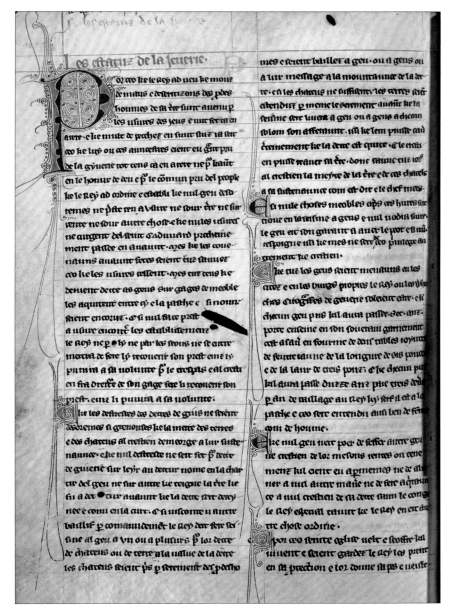

The Statute of the Jewry, 1275

usury to include any loan in which the amount to be repaid was greater than the original loan, and made it much harder for Jewish lenders to recover unpaid debts. They could no longer count on the king's assistance in pursuing tardy clients, who were now permitted to keep half their chattels and land rather than forfeiting them in full until the loan or interest due was repaid. Where the land had already been given or sold to a third party, this now had to be proved by the debtor in court. The Jews were, in addition, prohibited from pawnbroking, collecting interest on existing debts and inheriting debts from their heirs or tenants.[187] From now on, the king declared, the Jews must earn their living like Christians, by physical toil or trade. In reality for the vast majority, this was completely impossible.

Many of those whose livelihoods had previously relied on lending money, probably had no choice but to carry on doing so, with or without interest, relying on illicit pawnbroking and loans repayable from rent. Others went back to dealing in plate, bullion and perhaps foreign coin, with many resorting to storing capital in gold rings, silver vessels and stocks of broken silver. A few, like Benedict, became commodity brokers, buying up grain and wool on future purchases, and profiting by the difference between the purchase and selling price. But by the late 1270s, Jewish lending was a shadow of what it had been and was now overwhelmingly small-scale, rural, and short-term, much more similar to the type of moneylending carried out by Jews on the Continent.[188]

The 1275 Statute was the latest and by far the cruellest of a series of increasingly punitive laws enacted against the Jews. It marked an important and sinister change in the position of Jews in England, who were referred to for the first time as the king's 'serfs', and made clear that the king's protection was 'a matter of royal grace and favour, not something to which the Jews were entitled as of right as the King's subjects'.[189] The statute rang the death knell for the English Jewry. But it was death played out in slow motion, a long painful strangulation that would continue for another fifteen years, culminating in the mass expulsion of 1290.

Murder most foul

Licoricia was spared the misery of these final years, but her own ending was far from peaceful. One spring morning in 1277 she was found murdered on the floor of her house in Jewry Street.[190] Her Christian maid, Alice Bicton, lay dead close by, murdered alongside her mistress. Both

Licoricia and Alice had been killed by 'a blow to the chest made by a knife, to the heart'.[191] In other words, they were stabbed face-on and at very close quarters. Their bodies were discovered by Licoricia's daughter Belia, and the scene that greeted her that morning must have been gruesome and deeply shocking.[192] News of the murder was widely reported in England and even spread as far as Germany. The motive for the murder, however, was unclear, as was the identity of the culprit, even though the two women had been stabbed to death in the centre of town and in broad daylight.

Licoricia's sons, Isaac and Asher, promptly called for and paid for an official investigation. The first day of the inquest was a debacle. Not one member of the eighteen-person jury turned up and the sheriff had to be brought in to ensure attendance. Amongst those who did eventually show up were several guildsmen and old acquaintances of Licoricia's family. Several were officially meant to be the protectors of the Jews, not that this helped to secure justice for Licoricia and her family.

The chief suspects were three local men, but charges against all three were dropped and the blame was then pinned on a Winchester saddler named Ralph Le Seeler, who had conveniently vanished without trace. Ralph was pronounced guilty of killing Licoricia and her maid during a botched burglary attempt and was duly outlawed, a hollow sentence since he clearly had no intention of being found anywhere near Winchester. The city itself was heavily fined for not having done enough when the murders were first discovered, but no more was done to apprehend or punish the killer.

The inquiry into Licoricia's death bore all the hallmarks of a stitch-up. It was much less trouble for the jurors, who were mostly local bigwigs, to find a poor, insignificant and physically absent saddler guilty than to scrutinise too closely the activities of more influential and well-connected fellow-citizens. Cokerel and Asher were certainly not happy with the outcome. A year later they tried to bring a case against those originally suspected of killing their mother, but to no avail.[193]

After her death, Licoricia's house was sealed up to prevent anything in it being stolen or removed, but not long after the seals were broken and the property was comprehensively burgled. Five men were accused of the theft: the Sheriff of Hampshire, John of Havering, and two of his men, William of Chichester and Thomas de la Mare. In a bizarre new plot twist, two of Licoricia's own grandsons, Abraham and Lumbard, the sons of Benedict, were also charged. To make matters more complicated, Benedict had recently been put in charge of stamping out precisely the kind of misconduct of which his sons were now accused.

Charges against Lumbard were later dropped and John of Havering was cleared after managing to prove he had been in London at the time of the burglary. Havering, however, was 'a very shady character' who was frequently on the wrong side of the law and Abraham also had a long track record of criminality,[194] so although unlikely, it is not entirely implausible that they were acting in league. In the end, Abraham was found guilty and outlawed, along with Havering's two men, who had, like Ralph the saddler, already conveniently fled the city.

The coin-clipping disaster

Throughout the inquiries into his mother's death and the theft of her property, Benedict kept a very low profile. He had good reason not to want to get embroiled in local politics, having recently been appointed as escheator for the Jewry and Keeper of the Queen's Gold. On top of this, Benedict was dealing with serious problems of his own.

The financial restrictions imposed by the 1275 Statute of Jewry meant that many Jews were now struggling to earn even a meagre living. Conversions to Christianity soared after 1275, and many Jews were forced to turn to illegal ways to make money. One of these was coin-clipping. This involved trimming tiny pieces off the edges of coins (making them worth less than they should have been) and refashioning the trimmings into silver plate or other forms of silver, which were then sold on. Christians as well as Jews were involved in this illegal trade, and the practice was not new. Earlier in the century, Jewish financiers were so concerned about corrupted coinage that they paid for an investigation into coin-clipping and called for harsher penalties for offenders. One of the men leading this earlier investigation was David of Oxford.

Accusations of coin-clipping rose steeply after 1275, and within three years the situation had reached crisis point, with hundreds of Jews and Christians arrested on coin-clipping charges. The penalty, if found guilty, was execution. By 1278, in London alone, as many as 680 Jews were imprisoned awaiting trial, around a third of the country's total Jewish population. Entire families and even whole communities were arrested in some cases. Many people seem to have leapt at the chance to make false allegations as a way of settling old scores and giving vent to their prejudices against Jews and foreigners, and the properties of many imprisoned Jews were broken into and looted while their owners were awaiting trial. With prisons all over the country filled to bursting as the coin-clipping trials gathered pace, even the king's elephant house had to be requisitioned as a temporary prison. Prisoners had to pay for the cost of their fuel, food and blankets, and conditions were utterly wretched for the poorest, who in addition to cold and hunger were shackled together day and night. Those with the means to do so could pay for the privilege of better food and not to be fettered; some paid to be allowed out on day release. Those who could not afford these 'perks' were simply left to freeze and starve.

In January 1279, three groups of justices were authorised to try those accused. Although three times as many Christians were accused, when it came to actual executions, Jews outnumbered Christians ten to one, strongly suggesting that coin-clipping accusations and sentencing were not just part of a fiscal clean-up but an active mechanism for Jewish persecution[195] Official records of these trials have not survived, so precise information about the basis for sentencing and accurate numbers for those affected is not known, but at least 269 Jews were hanged on the basis of accusations against them and another 148 Jews are known to have been severely punished with the confiscation of all their property.[196] It has also come to light that, under the guise of buying up plate made from melted down silver for the treasury, agents of the king had been secretly gathering information on Jews potentially involved in coin-clipping and related activities even before the arrests began, in what one historian has described as a 'well-organized 'sting' operation'.[197] This information was then used as evidence in trials whose outcome was a foregone conclusion.

Sometime between 1278 and 1279, at the height of the arrests and trials, Benedict himself was arrested on coin-clipping charges, imprisoned in the Tower of London, quite probably in the room that had previously been his office as Keeper of the Queen's Gold. At trial he was found

View of the Tower of London, where Licoricia was imprisoned on four occasions, and her son Benedict was also imprisoned. The Tower did not look like this in their day.

guilty and subsequently hanged, one of 269 Jews put to death in the 'orgy of executions'.[198] In the patent rolls for January 1280, Benedict is referred to as 'sometime Jew of Winchester, hanged for felony'. In addition to his various properties, Benedict's goods and chattels were valued at £269 14s. 3½d., and included 168 silver spoons, 124 gold rings, 28 silk girdles, a silver cup and 49 'books of the law of the Jews'.[199] Others who lost their lives in the coin-clipping pogrom were Benedict's son, Lumbard, Deudonne the chirographer, and two of Belia of Bedford's sons, Benedict and Jacob.[200] No Jewish family in England was untouched by the coin-clipping disaster. Nearly all lost at least one family member, and in some cases whole families were executed.[201]

On 1 May 1279, King Edward finally called a halt to the trials and executions. A few days later, as if realising he had missed a trick, he ordered that those Jews not yet charged should not be charged, but could fine for their release. That is to say, even though charges had been dropped, all those still in prison had to pay to be let out. So many properties had been confiscated and looted while their owners were in prison that many emerged from prison to find themselves homeless and destitute.

The terrible cost to the Jews was a financial bonanza for the treasury. The value of all the Jewish property confiscated from those awaiting trial and those who had been executed amounted to an estimated £10,000, an enormous sum of money. Many others profited illegally by selling or keeping goods stolen from imprisoned or executed Jews. One of these was a former Jew and friend and business associate of Benedict's called Henry de Durngate, also known in the records as Henry of Winchester, who had converted to Christianity in 1252. Henry III had acted as his godfather, personally raising him from the baptismal font and then knighting him. De Durngate had been one of the Winchester guardians of the Jews, and he was a witness to Benedict's purchase of the Sutton Hundreds estate.

De Durngate appears to have been a slippery and unscrupulous character whose only real allegiance was to himself. He had served as a juror in Licoricia's murder inquiry in 1277, where his testimony did more to pervert the course of justice than to assist it: his evidence helped secure the release of the three men originally accused of her death. He also used his connections with members of the Jewish community to gather evidence against them in the mid 1270s ahead of the coin-clipping trials as part of a premeditated 'sting campaign' authorised by Edward I.[202] It has also been suggested that Edward I endowed de Durngate's evidence against the accused Jews with 'the force of record', making it in effect impossible to counter.[203] If this was the case, then de Durngate was directly responsible for the deaths and ruination of hundreds of his former co-religionists. He may well also have played a part in mounting a case against Benedict. He certainly showed no scruple in turning Benedict's death to his own advantage: after Benedict's execution, de Durngate took the opportunity to help himself to many of his former friend's belongings, as well as those of other condemned Jews. In 1279, he was arrested for possession of 'clothes, furs, books, copper lamps and girdles of silk in order to sell them', and fined 1,000 marks for holding back property belonging to the king and concealing the goods of 'the hanged Jew, Benedict of Winchester'.[204]

How could someone as successful and well-connected as Benedict have suffered such a sudden and catastrophic reversal of fortunes? In 1275 the queen had made him Keeper of the Queen's Gold, and as recently as 1277 the king had granted him a special licence to trade anywhere in the kingdom. Before the coin-clipping frenzy, Benedict had been able to count on several high-ranking patrons, who had helped him find ways round the tightening restrictions, yet not one of them was willing to come to his rescue after his arrest. His fate is a stark example of just how quickly patronage could melt away when it was no longer useful or politically wise for the patron. Even the most successful Jewish financiers were, in reality, always very vulnerable. Benedict, for one, had become more valuable dead than alive.

The road to expulsion

Decimated in number and financially ruined, daily life for the Jews was becoming less and less bearable. The last three decades of Henry III's reign had been disastrous for his Jewish subjects. Between 1240 and 1272, the size of the Jewry had shrunk from around 5,000 people to less than 3,000 as a result of 'ruinous royal taxation, civil war, mob violence, and judicial murder'.[205] The ruination of the Jewry may not have been the king's explicit intention but he had, nevertheless, 'presided over the effective bankrupting of the English Jewish community and a permanent reduction in its financial value to the crown.'[206]

A still darker legacy of Henry's reign stemmed from his personal attitude towards Jews and Judaism, which manifested most obviously in his regular confiscation of Jewish land and buildings,[207] his ardent support for Jewish conversion to Christianity,[208] [209] and his embrace of accusations of Jewish ritual murder. Henry's willingness to believe the ritual murder accusations was in part a product of his devotion to the Virgin Mary, since Marian piety at this time was strongly linked with associations of blood sacrifice and Jewish culpability for the death of Christ.[210]

In December 1243, Henry confiscated one of the synagogues in London to provide the hospital of St Anthony with a chapel dedicated to the Virgin Mary attached to the hospital. His personal intervention in the case of a murdered Christian child, Little Hugh of Lincoln, in 1255 had more immediately devastating consequences, leading to the execution of nineteen Jews, one in Lincoln and the rest in London, and the arrest of ninety others, all of whom were also sentenced to death but subsequently reprieved.[211] This was the first time a ruling monarch had publicly supported a blood libel.

Henry's active encouragement of conversions and his public endorsement of the Lincoln ritual murder accusation were highly unusual for rulers in his lifetime, but he established a dismal blueprint for many other monarchs to come, not least his son Edward.

The tomb of 'Little St Hugh' at Lincoln Cathedral. Hugh was found dead in 1255 and a blood libel fabricated against the Jews. Henry III personally intervened to execute Jews.

The hostile environment instituted by Edward I included strict new controls on where Jews could live and the wearing of the hated badge was enforced for every Jew over the age of six. Jews had been put under pressure to convert to Christianity throughout Henry III's reign, but this now intensified. An annual poll tax was introduced and applied to every person over the age of twelve to fund new houses for the converts, and the Jews were compelled by order of the king to attend services at which they were forced to listen to preachers urging conversion.[212]

Edward's attempt to stamp out moneylending was a spectacular failure, and in a draft document of 1283 he appears to have been considering reauthorising Jewish lending, although not without first blaming the Jews themselves for his lack of success, claiming that:

> ... by a new and wicked device, under colour of trading and good contracts and convenants ... by bonds and divers instruments ... in which [the Jews] stipulated for twice, thrice, or four times as much as they

part with to Christians in one and the same transaction of debt or
contract, avoiding the use of the term 'usury' by means of penalties,
whence only confusion, and the ruin of a great part of the people, and
the ultimate disherison of many can ensue.[213]

In the event, the ban on Jewish moneylending remained in place.[214] This
not only deprived the Crown of a source of income, it also resulted in a
sharp rise in the numbers of Christian moneylenders, who stepped in to
fill the void left by the dead or ruined Jews. While some Christians de-
plored the brutal treatment of the Jews, others were eager to profit by it
and Edward's wife, Eleanor of Castile, was one of the worst offenders. She
had close associations with Jewish moneylenders, including Benedict, and
she sometimes employed them as her private financiers, but she also ruthlessly exploited them to enhance her personal wealth.

Eleanor was entitled to claim 10 per cent of all Jewish fines, tallages
and confiscated property as the Queen's Gold, and she quickly persuaded
Edward to extend the terms to include 'the entire belongings of those who
were executed or had been allotted to her'.[215] She used the Keepers of the
Queen's Gold to rake in every possible penny. Jacob of Oxford served as
her Keeper until he went mad and died in 1276, whereupon Eleanor confiscated all his wealth and left his widow and children destitute. The ill-fated
Benedict was Jacob's replacement.

Despite her devout Christianity, Eleanor was equally ready and willing to benefit from moneylending. One of her favourite ways of feeding
her seemingly insatiable hunger for wealth was to cancel a debt owed to a
Jewish moneylender in exchange for the pledged estates of the Christian
debtor. While the debtor could now count on the queen's favour, the Jew
who had made the original loan was left with nothing at all. From 1274
to 1290 Eleanor took possession of estates worth more than £2,500 a year.
At other times she took over the debts and gave them to her favourites
as payments or gifts.[216] Even when the courts ruled that confiscated land
and debts should be reinstated, she simply ignored them. Sixty to seventy
wrongful land seizures were recorded.[217] So morally and legally scandalous
was Eleanor's conduct, the Archbishop of Canterbury repeatedly warned
her that her actions were endangering her immortal soul.[218]

Throughout the 1280s many Jews paid the necessary fines for permission to leave the country, and by 1289 most of the wealthiest had gone.[219] The majority of those who remained were the widows, elderly parents and children of those executed for coin-clipping. The Winchester Jewry, which had been hit hard by the deaths of Licoricia and Benedict, was now one of the poorest communities in the country. By 1285 only four Winchester Jews were still liable to pay tax, one of whom was Licoricia's youngest son Asher. By this time King Edward may have already decided that his next step *vis-à-vis* the Jews would be mass expulsion.

The year 1287 was bookended by terrible storms. In February, hundreds of people lost their lives when the south coast was engulfed by a storm of such ferocity that whole areas of the coastline were transformed. Seaside towns found themselves landlocked and inland towns found themselves surrounded by water. In December, a second massive storm surged through the North Sea, killing five hundred people in East Anglia alone.

Between these two natural disasters, the Jewry was engulfed by catastrophe of a different kind: the king imposed a new – and as it would turn out final – tallage of £12,000, a ludicrously high sum considering the Jews' impoverished state by this time. Less than £5,000 was raised and on 2 May, the entire Jewry was taken hostage to compel them to pay whatever they could.

Imprisoned in Winchester Castle, Licoricia's youngest son, Asher, scratched a Hebrew inscription into the stone wall of his prison cell recording the date and time of the arrests, and his name: 'On Friday, eve of the Sabbath in which the pericope Emor is read, all the Jews of the isle were imprisoned. I, Asser, inscribed this ...' Discovered in the seventeenth century and translated by the Hebraist John Selden, only this small fragment of the inscription has survived, but Asher's words powerfully underscore the indignities suffered by the Anglo-Jewry at the hands of the English Crown.

The words 'On Friday, eve of the Sabbath in which the pericope Emor is read' do not simply provide the date and time of the arrest. Asher is also recording for posterity that the mass imprisonment of his people took place when they were all gathered in synagogue for Friday evening prayers at the start of the Sabbath, as the authorities would have known and ruthlessly chose to exploit. The timing of the arrests was not just a

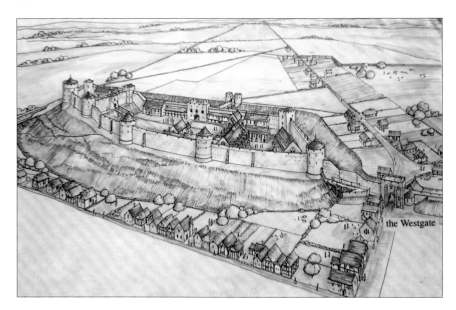

Reconstruction of Winchester Castle, c. 1283, at its height after Henry III's renovations. Asher was imprisoned in its 'Jews' Tower'. The Jewish cemetery can be found to the west of the castle, at the top of the illustration, and the town is to the east.

shameful offence against fairness and custom. Observing the Sabbath was a sacred injunction, given directly from God to Moses at Mount Sinai (a reminder of which was sewn on to the garments of Asher and his co-religionists in the form of the detested *tabula* badge). By arresting the Jews on the Sabbath, the Christians were profaning God's law and forcing the Jews themselves to profane it.

Asher's reference to 'the pericope Emor' is also worth closer attention. *Emor* (Leviticus 21:1–24:23) was the biblical portion read aloud in all synagogues on that particular weekend in 1287. It includes an explicit reminder of God's commandment to the people of Israel to observe the Sabbath as a day 'of solemn rest, a holy convocation'.[220] Equally pertinent are the concluding verses of *Emor*, which address the issue of punishments for blasphemy, murder, injuring one's fellow or destroying his property, and which contain the famous lines: 'And if a man maim his neighbour, as he hath done, so shall it be done to him, breach for breach, eye for eye, tooth for tooth; as he hath maimed a man, so shall it be rendered unto him.' (Leviticus 24:19–20)

Asher's inscription is a rare instance of a medieval English Jew speaking directly to us across the centuries, all the more poignant because *emor* is Hebrew for 'speaks'. This is forty-four-year-old Asher speaking out, and his rage and despair are still audible hundreds of years later. His mother had been murdered in her own home, his brother and nephew had been executed, and his people had been subjected to repeated attacks and slanders, systematically reduced to poverty, and now imprisoned *en masse* while at prayer on their holy Sabbath, stripped of their liberty and facing another punitive demand for money. What was going through Asher's mind as he scratched his message to the future? Was he appealing to the Jews to keep faith and hold to their religious tenets in the face of these repeated outrages against them? Was he wondering in anguish whether they in some way deserved their atrocious treatment for failing in their religious observances? Or was he calling for divine or human retribution for the offences he and his fellow Jews had suffered, invoking God's words in the penultimate verse of *Emor*: 'You shall have one manner of law, as well for the stranger as for the home-born; for I am the LORD your God.'

It was not only Asher's writing on the wall by this time. That same year, King Edward announced the expulsion of Jews from the province of Gascony in France, then held by England.[221] The following year, in December 1289, two more regions of France, Maine and Anjou, which belonged to Charles II, King of Sicily, expelled all Jews from these territories.[222] A year later, it was the turn of the English Jews.

On 18 June 1290, the sheriffs of the counties of England were ordered to seal the *archae* at the end of the month. No explanation was given, but the purpose of the order became clear the following month, on 18 July, when the king issued writs to the sheriffs that all the Jews of the realm were to leave the country on pain of death before the Christian feast of All Saints, 1 November.

The Edict of Expulsion stipulated that the Jews were not to be harmed and must be allowed safe conduct to leave the country 'provided that before they leave they restore the pledges of Christians in their possession to those to whom they belong'.[223] These instructions did not deter everyone. A shipload of Jewish exiles, who had been encouraged to disembark temporarily on a sandbank in the Thames estuary, were refused back on board

fcripta quazdā lttāz que in theſauria nta

The Expulsion of the Jews from England. Detail from the Rochester Chronicle, 14th century

when the tide flowed back in and were told by the ship's captain, Henry Adrian, to save themselves by parting the water and walking to safety like Moses. All of them were left to drown, while Adrian absconded with their possessions. Something similar occurred to the ill-fated passengers of another ship, intercepted by the authorities off the coast of Burnham in Norfolk. The crew were nowhere to be seen, and the sole surviving passenger on board was one Jewish boy. A third disaster befell a group of Jewish passengers who embarked at Broomhill in Kent. Soon after setting sail, the ship was boarded and the Jews robbed of their meagre possessions. The crew then forced the Jewish passengers to disembark at low tide on a sandbank three miles offshore called Jury's Gap, where they were abandoned to their fate.[224]

The exiled Jews were allowed to take with them only the cash and personal belongings in their possession. What little was left of their bonds and property reverted to the Crown. It is likely that some of their belongings were left in the safekeeping of Christians or converted Jews, or hidden in the hope of being retrieved at a later date, as happened in the case of precious items belonging to the Jewish communities of Erfurt in Germany and Colmar in Alsace during pogroms in the fourteenth century. The Bodleian Bowl, given to the Jews of Colchester by Rabbi Joseph in 1260, may likewise have been hidden in the hope of later retrieval because it somehow ended up in a moat in Norwich and was only discovered in the seventeenth century.

By 26 November 1290, all twenty of the *archae* from the remaining Jewries had been delivered to London, the Jews were gone, and two hundred years of Jewish life in England had come to an end. Amongst the exiles were Licoricia's sons, Asher and Lumbard, and her grandchildren.

England was the first country in Europe to evict its entire Jewish population and it paved the way for others to do the same in the decades and centuries that followed. Why Edward took this extreme step is contested. The official reason, made much of by the king, was that the Expulsion Decree was punishment for the continuation of Jewish moneylending. The real reasons were more complex. Stripped of their assets, utterly impoverished and reduced at best to illicit small-scale lending to peasants and craftsmen, the Jews were no longer of much economic value to the king or his land-hungry courtiers, making it unlikely that the decision to force out what remained of the Jewry was purely motivated by hope of monetary gain.[225] Politics, religion and prevailing social attitudes probably played a much bigger part.

Edward by this time was dealing with serious territorial conflicts with the Scots, and expelling the Jews may have helped him to secure the barons' military support in fighting these campaigns. Parliament, always jealous of the king's access to funds from Jewish tallage and enterprise, also indicated that it would offer a financial lifeline in return for the eviction of the Jews. Rising anti-Jewish sentiment, both in society generally and from the upper echelons of the Church, was another significant influence on Edward. So too was the renewed interest by the late thirteenth century in the forging of an English identity, a project begun by Simon de Montfort and which may have contributed to hostility to people seen as 'foreign' in any way.

Another factor in Edward's decision was his religious convictions, shared and encouraged by his wife, Eleanor of Castile, and his mother, Eleanor of Provence. Both of these powerful women had in earlier times been willing to work closely with individual Jewish financiers and had personally profited from their loans, but by the 1280s both had become openly hostile to Jews. In 1275, Eleanor of Provence, with her son's agreement, had expelled the Jews from all the towns in her gift, banishing them from Gloucester, Worcester, Cambridge, Bath, Guildford, Andover, and Marlborough, where Licoricia's son Asher was then living.

Edward's wife, Eleanor of Castile, in particular may well have been a driving force behind the 1290 Edict of Expulsion. The Benedictines, to whom Eleanor was devoted, and the Dominicans certainly played their part in the development of anti-Jewish ideology and discourse during the twelfth and thirteenth centuries. Matthew Paris, for instance, the most explicitly antisemitic of the thirteenth-century chroniclers, was attached to the Benedictine abbey at St Albans. But it was the Franciscans who exerted the greatest influence at Edward I's court and who favoured expulsion of Jews from Christian territories over forced conversion.[226] Queen Eleanor is known to have had trusted spiritual and political Franciscan advisors.[227]

By early 1290 it was clear that Eleanor was dying, and she was perhaps for the first time seriously contemplating the state of her soul, fully aware that profiting from moneylending was a mortal sin in the eyes of her religion.[228] She may have urged the expulsion of the Jews as a last chance to obtain moral expiation for some of her earthly sins. If this was her dying wish, her distraught husband Edward could hardly refuse, for he had assisted and enabled her financial rapacity. Eleanor died on 28 November 1290, just four weeks after the last English Jews left the kingdom.

Licoricia's own death in 1277 at least spared her from the horrors that engulfed her children and grandchildren, along with so many other members of the Jewry. The misery of those final years was powerfully captured by the Norfolk rabbi, Meir of Norwich, in poems discovered six centuries later in the Vatican Library in Rome.[229] Despair battles with hope in Meir's words, which articulate both his anguish at the terrible suffering of his people and his passionate faith in God to provide them with the inner strength to endure these trials:

> *In the land of the heavy-hearted and exhausted*
> *We have heard the people's reproach.*
> *Silently we await the light.*

Majestic are you and luminous
You irradiate our darkness with light.
They make heavy our yoke,
They are finishing us off.
They repeat 'Let us scorn them!'
Until the light.
Majestic are you and luminous
You irradiate our darkness with light.

(from 'Put a Curse on My Enemies')[230]

Rabbi Meir's words could serve equally well as a response to Jewish suffering in many other times and places across the centuries. But it should never be forgotten that they were first set down in response to the persecution the Jews experienced in medieval England.

Aftermath

The exiled Jews went to France and the German Rhineland, or settled in parts of eastern Europe that were then welcoming Jews forced out of other places.[231] A handful remained in England as converts to Christianity. The economic gaps left by the Jews were soon filled by Christian traders and moneylenders. Jewish properties and belongings, meanwhile, were put up for sale, with many of the best houses being given by King Edward to his friends, royal favourites and influential clergymen. In Oxford, all the houses previously owned by Jews were given to the king's relative, William Burnell.[232] In Huntington the *scola* was turned into a monastery, and the house it was attached to became a gaol. The monks were far from pleased when they discovered they could only reach their monastery by going through the gaol. Books that had been the prized possessions of the Jews of Cambridgeshire were flogged at auction and bought up cheap, 'gold for brass' as one buyer put it.[233]

In Winchester, the expulsion hastened the city's economic decline. Jewry Street and Fleshmonger Street (now St Peter's Street), where many Jews had lived, fell into a state of neglect. By 1300, the grounds of the royal palace were being used as a market for cattle, corn and wood, as well as overspill from the cathedral cemetery. Winchester's medieval heyday had outlasted the Jews by just twelve years. The famous Round Table, made for the great tournament Edward held at Winchester in April 1290 to celebrate the forthcoming marriages of his children, Margaret, Joan, and Edward, was intended as a symbol of England's greatness, but it must also be seen as a reminder of England's appalling treatment of its Jewish community.

Anti-Jewish sentiment did not end with the expulsion. In the fourteenth and fifteenth centuries, accusations of host desecration by Jews proliferated and Christian miracle stories, illuminated manuscripts and popular medieval stage plays stoked memories of alleged ritual murders by Jews in earlier centuries. Many of the negative associations and beliefs about Jews that subsequently took hold and played out in Europe with such terrible consequences in later generations, such as mass expulsions, massacres, looting of Jewish property, repressive legislation and the blood libel, were common and widespread in medieval England. Like other minority groups in more recent history, Jews in England were used in ways that do not reflect well on those in power.

Just as so many great eighteenth and early nineteenth century institutions in England were founded on profits from slavery, so were many of the magnificent English medieval churches and cathedrals built with money extorted from Jews. Just as the Windrush generation in the twentieth century were encouraged to immigrate to England and then brutally forced to leave once their usefulness was over, so Jews in medieval England were courted, exploited and then discarded. Just as many Jews in Nazi Germany in the 1930s were driven from their country by tightening restrictions that made daily life unendurable and dangerous, so Jews in medieval England were legislated against and persecuted between 1260 and 1290.[234] The long view of English history makes clear that antisemitism was not something that only or even mainly happened somewhere else.

But it would be wrong to view the Jews of medieval England simply as passive victims, any more than it would be to see them as the hard-hearted moneylenders of antisemitic caricature. Many historical accounts before the mid-twentieth century were tinged if not thoroughly tainted with anti-Jewish prejudices, some of which still linger in contemporary assumptions and attitudes. Seen through this distorting lens, medieval Jews have for too long been assumed by some to have been more powerful than they really were, and by others as so marginal that they can be ignored as irrelevant. Neither of these portrayals is accurate. Even the most prosperous and powerful members of the Jewish community were always operating in a highly volatile and precarious world.[235]

As Licoricia's story amply demonstrates, patronage and favour could be withdrawn from one day to the next; loans, pledges and property could be confiscated and annulled at any moment; tax demands could wipe out fortunes overnight; and violence could erupt without warning. Within the parameters of these highly challenging conditions, the Jewry also had to manage its own internal affairs, needs and disputes. Individual Jews, such as Licoricia and Benedict, were clearly of financial importance both locally and nationally, but as one historian has pointed out, 'what is remarkable about them is how they survived, through a mixture of skill and good fortune, so long'.[236]

Jews in medieval England were always only a tiny minority group, but they played their part in the country's development during the two hundred years they lived there before the 1290 expulsion. Their identities, distinctive personalities and diverse experiences have been largely airbrushed from history, but they were never a homogenous group who all thought, lived and behaved alike. Small in number and with its own distinctive religious beliefs and customs, the medieval Jewry was nevertheless made up of individuals who were as personally diverse as any other group of human beings.

Licoricia was undoubtedly one of the Jewry's most remarkable members. As a wife, as a mother, as an inhabitant of Winchester, as a businesswoman and financier, she lived a long and full life with energy, determination, resilience and success. A woman of worth in many senses of the word, Licoricia merits remembrance and as the *eschet chayil* aptly concludes: 'Let her enjoy the benefits of the affluence she has amassed, and at the same time let her be praised for what she has achieved.'[237]

Acknowledgements

A number of individuals and organisations have helped to bring this book into being. I wish to acknowledge the Licoricia of Winchester Appeal for commissioning and publishing this volume with generous financial support from the Arts Council of England, the Jewish Historical Society of England, and many others. For invaluable historical advice and feedback on the manuscript, I am indebted to Hester Abrams, Anna Sapir Abulafia, Abigail Green, Pam Manix, Emily Rose, Miri Rubin, Norman Solomon and Robert Stacey. I would like to thank William Carver for pointing me in the direction of useful preliminary research material and for his help in identifying and sourcing images for the book. I would also like to thank Stephen O'Connell and Dickon Kelly who went out of their way to share their knowledge about the Chapel of the Holy Sepulchre in Winchester Cathedral.

An essential starting point for my research into Licoricia's life and the Winchester Jewry was Suzanne Bartlet's, *Licoricia of Winchester: Marriage, Motherhood and Murder*. Bartlet tragically died in 2012, but her scholarly dedication to expanding knowledge of Licoricia deserves to be recognised, not least for helping to pave the way for the work of the Licoricia of Winchester Appeal, which has in turn done so much to raise public awareness and understanding of this remarkable medieval woman. Besides its many other activities, the Licoricia of Winchester Appeal charity enabled both this publication and the magnificent statue of Licoricia by sculptor Ian Rank-Broadley FRSS, which now graces Jewry Street in Winchester.

Writing books is an arduous and frequently solitary journey, and this one was no exception. For their support, succour and company along the way, and generally keeping me sane and smiling, I am hugely grateful to Gabriel Amherst, Sally Bayley, Penny Boreham, Rebecca Carter, Kate Clanchy, Abigail Green, Andrew Fingret, Rebecca Gowers, Alice Jolly,

Stephen Kinsella and Sally Paskett. Written during the locked-down months of the coronavirus pandemic, the book – and Licoricia – were an inescapable part of daily life whether they liked it or not for those locked-down with me. For their unfailing patience and love throughout, my deepest gratitude to Jessie Slim, Solomon Slim and Jeremy Arden.

The Licoricia of Winchester Appeal

The aims of the publisher, The Licoricia Of Winchester Appeal, are to use the sculpture of Licoricia of Winchester, this book, and lessons for schools, to educate the public about Winchester's long-forgotten medieval Jewish community and its Royal medieval past, to promote tolerance and diversity, to inspire women and young people, and to enhance the city.

The Licoricia of Winchester Appeal is deeply grateful to its many donors, including:

Alex Habel
Andrew and Juliet Wilkinson
Caroline and Charles Gregson
David and Lindsay Levin
David Uri Charitable Trust
Garfield Weston Foundation
GS Plaut Charitable Trust Limited
Jenny Nathan
John Hall
Jonathan and Sarah Bayliss
Jonathan Wolf-Phillips
Kim and Nicky Gottlieb
Leslie Bartlet
Malcolm Brown
Mark Clarfelt
Mark Lewisohn
Michael and Erin Cohen
Paul Seftel
Raymond Dwek
Rubin Foundation Charitable Trust

Rupert and Elizabeth Nabarro Charitable Trust
Sam and Rosie Berwick
Siena Golan
Stuart and Bianca Roden
The 29th May 1961 Charitable Trust
The Alan and Sheila Diamond Charitable Trust
The Arts Council, England
The Aurelius Charitable Trust
The Brilliant family
The Charlotte Bonham-Carter Charitable Trust
The City of Winchester Trust
The Habel family
The Harold Hyam Wingate Foundation
The Hobson Charity
The Hollick Family Charitable Trust
The Jewish Historical Society of England
The Oak Foundation Ltd
The Pattisson family
The Phillips Family Charitable Trust
The Thornton Trust
Tony and Andy Stoller
William and Francheska Pattisson
William and Maggie Carver

Selected Bibliography

Abrams, Rebecca, *The Jewish Journey: 4000 Years in 22 Objects* (Oxford: Ashmolean, 2017).

Abrams, Rebecca and Merchan-Hamann, Cesar, eds, *Jewish Treasures of Oxford Libraries* (Oxford: Bodleian Libraries, 2020).

Baker, Darren, *With All for All: The Life of Simon de Montfort* (Stroud: Amberley Publishing, 2015).

Baker, Darren, *Simon de Montfort and the Rise of the English Nation* (Stroud: Amberley Publishing, 2018).

Bale, Anthony, 'Fictions of Judaism in England Before 1290', in Patricia Skinner, ed., *Jews in Medieval Britain: Historical, Literary and Archaeological Perspectives* (Woodbridge: Boydell, 2003).

Bale, Anthony, 'Afterword: Violence, Memory and the Traumatic Middle Ages', in Sarah Rees Jones and Sethina Watson, eds, *Christians and Jews in Angevin England: The York Massacre of 1190, Narratives and Contexts* (York: York Medieval Press, 2013).

Bartlet, Suzanne, 'Three Jewish Businesswomen in Thirteenth-Century Winchester', *Jewish Culture and History*, 3/2 (2000), 31–54.

Bartlet, Suzanne, 'Women in the Medieval Anglo-Jewish Community', in Patricia Skinner, ed., *Jews in Medieval Britain: Historical, Literary and Archaeological Perspectives* (Woodbridge: Boydell, 2003).

Bartlet, Suzanne, *Licoricia of Winchester: Marriage, Motherhood and Murder in the Medieval Anglo-Jewish Community*, ed. Patricia Skinner (Elstree: Vallentine Mitchell & Co Ltd, 2009).

Baskin, Judith R., ed., 'Jewish Women in the Middle Ages', in *Jewish Women in Historical Perspective* (Detroit: Wayne State University Press, 1991), 109–14.

Berman Brown, Reva and McCartney, Sean, 'David of Oxford and Licoricia of Winchester: Glimpses into a Jewish Family in Thirteenth-Century England', *Jesish Historical Studies*, 39 (2004), 1–35.

Biddle, Martin, ed., *Winchester in the Early Middle Ages* (Oxford: Clarendon Press, 1976)

Brand, Paul, 'Jews and the Law in England, 1275–1290', *The English Historical Review*, Vol. 115, No. 464 (Nov., 2000)

Brand, Paul, 'The Jewish Community of England in the Records of the English Royal Government', in Patricia Skinner, ed., *Jews in Medieval Britain: Historical, Literary and Archaeological Perspectives* (Woodbridge: Boydell, 2003), 73.

Carpenter, David, *The Struggle for Mastery: The Penguin History of Britain 1066–1284* (London: Penguin, 2004).

Carpenter, David, *Henry III: 1207–1258 (The English Monarchs Series): The Rise to Power and Personal Rule, 1207–1258* (New Haven, CT: Yale University Press, 2020).

Clanchy, Michael, *England and its Rulers: 1066–1307*, 4th edn (Hoboken, NJ: Wiley-Blackwell, 2014).

Cohen, Jeffrey J., 'The Flow of Blood in Norwich', *Speculum*, 79/1 (2004), 26–65.

Dobson, R. B., *The Jews of Medieval York and the Massacre of March 1190* (York: Borthwick Institute Publications, 1974).

Edwards, John, 'The Church and the Jews in Medieval England', in Patricia Skinner, ed., *Jews in Medieval Britain: Historical, Literary and Archaeological Perspectives*, (Woodbridge: Boydell, 2003).

Einbinder, Susan L., 'Meir b. Elijah of Norwich: Persecution and Poetry Among Medieval English Jews', *Journal of Medieval History*, 26/2 (2000), 145–62.

Elman, P., 'The Economic Causes of the Expulsion of the Jews in 1290', *Economic History Review*, 7/1 (1936), 145.

Goldy, Charlotte N., 'Muriel, a Jew of Oxford: Using the Dramatic to Understand the Mundane in Anglo-Norman Towns', in Charlotte Newman Goldy and Amy Livingstone, eds, *Writing Medieval Women's Lives* (New York: Palgrave Macmillan, 2012), 227–45.

Hatot, Nicholas and Olszowy-Schlanger, Judith, eds, *Savants and Croyants: Les Juifs d'Europe du Nord au Moyen Age* (Gent: Snoeck, 2018).

Hillaby, Joe, 'London: the 13th-Century Jewry Revisited', *Jewish Historical Studies*, 23 (1990–92), 89–159.

Hillaby, Joe, 'Jewish Colonisation in the Twelfth Century', in Patricia Skinner, ed., *Jews in Medieval Britain: Historical, Literary and Archaeological Perspectives* (Woodbridge: Boydell, 2003).

Hillaby, Joe and Hillaby, Caroline, *The Palgrave Dictionary of Medieval Anglo-Jewish History* (London: Palgrave Macmillan, 2013).

Hoyle, Victoria, 'The Bonds that Bind: Money Lending Between Anglo-Jewish and Christian Women in the Plea Rolls of the Exchequer of the Jews, 1218–1280', *Journal of Medieval History*, 34 (2008), 119–129.

Hunt, Edwin S. and Murray, James M., *A History of Business in Medieval Europe, 1200–1550* (Cambridge: Cambridge University Press, 1999), 30.

Huscroft, Richard, *Expulsion: England's Jewish Solution* (Stroud: Tempus, 2006), 156–57.

Julius, Anthony, *Trials of the Diaspora: A History of Anti-Semitism in England* (Oxford: Oxford University Press, 2010).

Keene, Derek, *Survey of Medieval Winchester: Part I, II & III (in two volumes): Pt.1 & 2 (Winchester Studies 2)* (Oxford: Oxford University Press, 1985).

Krummel, Miriamne A., *Crafting Jewishness in Medieval England: Legally Absent, Virtually Present* (New York: Palgrave Macmillan, 2011).

Krummel, Miriamne A., 'Jewish Culture and Literature in England', in *Handbook of Medieval Culture, Vol. 2* (Berlin: De Gruyter, 2015).

Kushner, Tony, 'Winchester – Constructing the City of Memories' in Tony Kushner, *Anglo-Jewry Since 1066: Place, Locality and Memory* (Manchester: Manchester University Press, 2008).

Lipman, V. D., *The Jews of Medieval Norwich* (London: Jewish Historical Society 1967).

Lipton, Sara, 'Jewish Money and the Jewish Body in Medieval Iconography', in *Jews, Money, Myth* (London: Jewish Museum, London and Pears Institute for the Study of Antisemitism, Birkbeck University of London, 2019).

Mell, Julie, *The Myth of the Medieval Jewish Moneylender: Volume II: 2* (Palgrave Studies in Cultural and Intellectual History) (New York: Palgrave Macmillan, 2017).

Mell, Julie, *The Myth of the Medieval Jewish Moneylender: Volume I* (Palgrave Studies in Cultural and Intellectual History) (New York: Palgrave Macmillan, 2018).

Mell, Julie, 'The Myth of the Jewish Moneylender', in *Jews, Money, Myth* (London: Jewish Museum, London and Pears Institute for the Study of Antisemitism, Birkbeck University of London, 2019).

Mundill, Robin R., *England's Jewish Solution: Experiment and Expulsion*, 1262–1290 (Cambridge: Cambridge University Press, 1998).

Mundill, Robin R., *The King's Jews: Money, Massacre and Exodus in Medieval England* (New York: Continuum, 2010).

Mundill, Robin R., 'Edward I and the Final Phase of Anglo-Jewry', in Patricia Skinner, (ed.) *Jews in Medieval Britain: Historical, Literary and Archaeological Perspectives*, (Woodbridge: Boydell, 2003).

Berachiah haNaqdan, *Mishlei shu'alim [Fox Fables]*, tr. Moses Hadas (Jaffrey, NH, 2001).

Olszowy-Schlanger, Judith, 'Hebrew and Hebrew-Latin Documents from Medieval England: a Diplomatic and Palaeographical Study', *Jewish Historical Studies*, 51/1 (2016).

Paris, Matthew, *English History from the Year 1235 to 1273. Vol. III* (1854; New York, 1968).

Pim, Keiron, *Into the Light: The Medieval Hebrew Poetry of Meir of Norwich*, tr. Ellman Crasnow and Bente Elsworth, ed. and intro. (Norwich: East Publishing, 2013).

Richardson, H. G., *The English Jewry Under Angevin Kings* (London: Methuen, 1960).

Rose, E. M., *The Murder of William of Norwich: the Origins of the Blood Libel in Medieval Europe* (Oxford: Oxford University Press, 2015).

Roth, Cecil, *A History of the Jews in England* (Oxford: Clarendon Press, 1941).

Skinner, Patricia, ed., *Jews in Medieval Britain: Historical, Literary and Archaeological Perspectives* (Woodbridge: Boydell, 2003).

Stacey, Robert C., 'Royal Taxation and the Social Structure of Medieval Anglo-Jewry: the Tallages of 1239–1242', *Hebrew Union College Annual*, 56 (1985), 195–249.

Stacey, Robert C., *Politics, Policy and Finance Under Henry III, 1216–1245* (Oxford: Clarendon Press, 1987).

Stacey, Robert C., 'The Conversion of Jews to Christianity in Thirteenth-Century England', *Speculum*, 67/2 (1992), 263–83.

Stacey, Robert C., 'Jewish Lending and the Medieval English Economy', in Richard H. Britnell and Bruce M. S. Campbell, eds, *A Commercialising Economy, England 1086 to c. 1300* (Manchester: Manchester University Press, 1995).

Stacey, Robert C., 'The English Jews Under Henry III', in Patricia Skinner, ed., *Jews in Medieval Britain: Historical, Literary and Archaeological Perspectives* (Woodbridge: Boydell, 2003).

Stacey, Robert C., 'King Henry III and the Jews', in Kristine T. Utterback and Merrall L. Price, eds, *Jews in Medieval Christendom: 'Slay Them Not'* (Leiden: Brill, 2013).

Stacey, Robert C., 'The Massacres of 1189–90 and the Origins of the Jewish Exchequer, 1186–1226', in Sarah Rees Jones and Sethina Watson, eds, *Christians and Jews in Angevin England: The York Massacre of 1190, Narratives and Contexts* (York: York Medieval Press, 2013).

Tallan, Cheryl, 'The Economic Productivity of Medieval Jewish Widows', *Proceedings of the Eleventh World Congress of Jewish Studies*, 9 vols (Jerusalem, 1994) division B, vol. 2, 151–8.

Vincent, Nicholas, *Peter des Roches: An Alien in English Politics 1205–1238* (Cambridge: Cambridge University Press, 1996).

Wilkinson, Louise J., *Eleanor de Montfort: A Rebel Countess in Medieval England* (New York: Continuum, 2012).

Wilkinson, Louise J., *The Household Roll of Eleanor de Montfort*, British Library, Additional MS 8877: 63 (Publications of the Pipe Roll Society New Series, 63), (Woodbridge: Boydell and Brewer, 2020).

Picture Credits

The publisher would like to thank the following sources for supplying the illustrations for the book:

(Psalter of Henry of Blois, Psalter of St. Swithun Winchester, between 1121 and 1161); 23 (bottom) by the kind permission of the Chapter of Winchester Cathedral; 25 reproduced by kind permission of the Syndics of Cambridge University Library, (Taylor Schechter Collection TS.K.S.10); 28 The Bodleian Libraries, University of Oxford, MS Bodley Or. 62 fol. 3v; 30 After Map 6, *Winchester* c. 1300, first published in the British Historic Towns Atlas Volume VI, *Winchester* © Historic Towns Trust and Winchester Excavations Committee 2017;   32 Ivan Vdovin/Alamy; 33 © Historic England Archive; 34 by the kind permission of the Chapter of Winchester Cathedral; 36 (top) © Winchester Excavations Committee 2012; 36 (bottom) © Richard Croft; 39 © Jewish Museum London; 42 with kind permission of Dave Stewart, Friends of St Giles Hill Graveyeard www.stgileshill.org.uk;   44 Oxford Archaeology; 45 © British Library Board. All Rights Reserved/Bridgeman Images (The Golden Haggadah. Catalonia, early 14th century, The British Library, Eger.1070. Folio No: 5); 46 AN2009.10 The Bodleian Bowl. Image © Ashmolean Museum, University of Oxford; ; 48 by permission of the artist, Lucille Dweck; 51 The Great Hall, Winchester © Hampshire County Council; 56 with the kind permission of Wendy Bramall; 57 © B. Stefan, Thüringisches Landesamt für Denkmalpflege und Archäologie, Weimar; 59 The Warden and Fellows of Merton College, Oxford, (MCR 188); 62 with the kind permission of the Chapter of Westminster Abbey; 67 The National Archives, (E210/284); 69 © Historic England Archive; 71 Iona Wolff, @ionawolff-photo; 74 © British Library Board. All Rights Reserved/Bridgeman Images (The British Library, Cotton Nero D. II, f.177); 76 By the kind permission of Michelle Andrews; 79 The National Archives, (E 164/9, fol. 31v.3); 84 D-Stanley; 87 The Dean and Chapter of Lincoln Cathedral, photographer Jori Malinowski; 90 with the kind permission of Hampshire Cultural Trust; 92 © British Library Board. All Rights Reserved/Bridgeman Images (detail from the Rochester Chronicle, 14th century, The British Library, Cotton Nero D. II., folio 180.)

Endnotes

1   Proverbs 31:10–32 is known in Hebrew as *eshet chayil*, from the first two words, meaning 'a woman of worth'. The poem is a twenty-two-verse acrostic, with each verse starting with the letters of the Hebrew alphabet from aleph on. It is traditionally recited before *kiddush*, after the candles have been lit and before the meal is eaten.

2   As Robert Alter points out, the word *chayil* is a martial term, more typically applied to men than women, and relates to ideas of 'vigour', 'strength' and 'substance'. The poem suggests that these qualities are also required in the domestic and civic sphere, as admirable on the home front as on the battlefield. Robert Alter, *The Hebrew Bible: A Translation with Commentary, Vol III the Writings* (W.W. Norton & Company, 2018) 451.

3   Licoricia's date of birth is not known, nor do we know her age when she died, but we can make an educated guess. We know that she was widowed for the first time between 1225 and 1234, and that she and her first husband had three or four children, one of whom had reached adulthood by 1234. In 1242 or 1243 she had a fifth and as far as we know final child, her son Asher. Jewish women married young in medieval Europe, but the average age of menopause was similar to today, i.e. fifty, and fertility declines with age, so we can plausibly assume that Licoricia was between thirty-five and forty-three years old in 1243, when she gave birth to Asher. This would put her date of birth between 1200 and 1208, and her age at death between seventy-two and seventy-seven. Average life expectancy in thirteenth-century England was thirty-five. (Darrel W. Amundsen and Carol Jean Diers, 'The Age of Menopause in Medieval Europe', *Human Biology*, 45/4 (1973), 605–612. JSTOR, www.jstor.org/stable/41459908.)

4   Fiore et al., 'A History of the Therapeutic Use of Liquorice in Europe', *Journal of Ethnopharmacology*, August 2005. DOI: 10.1016/j.jep.2005.04.015, Source: PubMed.

5   The precise number and birth order of Licoricia's children is disputed. We know for sure that she had four sons, Cokerel, Benedict, Lumbard and Asher. Reference is made to a daughter named Belia in documents relating to Licoricia's death, but this may in reality have been a daughter-in-law or grand-daughter. She may have had other children besides this who did not survive to adulthood, or whose names do not appear in the official records.

6   Court clerks were not always fully literate or wholly reliable. Names of people and places were sometimes spelled differently within the same sentence, and if a case went on for a long time and different clerks recorded the proceedings, a person's gender could sometimes change too (Bartlet and Skinner, 2009, 5–10).

7   Various arguments have been put forward to explain the absence of Jews in England before the Norman Conquest. Stacey argues that Jewish traders were peripheral

to the economic transformation of early eleventh-century England and were therefore of little interest to the Anglo-Saxon kings of England, since they were neither part of the eleventh-century wool trade between Flanders and England nor the English trade in silver, gold, silk and spices with northern Italy. 'The Anglo-Saxon kings did not need them, and the Anglo-Saxon merchants of London probably did not want them as competitors. Jews may thus have been kept out of Anglo-Saxon England by deliberate royal decision.' (Stacey, 1995)

8   Stacey (1995, 82).

9   A second generation of Jewish immigrants arrived from France in 1096, possibly after attacks on the Rouen Jewry by Crusaders (Hillaby and Hillaby, 2013, 330–331).

10   Normandy had remained 'on the fringes' of the economic boom of northern Europe in the eleventh century, which was driven by the Rhineland silver trade. England, by contrast, had benefited greatly from the burgeoning new trade routes this silver facilitated. By conquering England, Normandy became 'a fully integrated part of this northern monetary and commercial world' (Stacey, 1995, 82).

11   According to Stacey (1995, 80–81), the dukes of Normandy may have encouraged the growth of the Jewish community in Rouen in the eleventh century because it offered links to the burgeoning Rhineland silver trade, as well as the established Mediterranean and North African trade in luxury goods.

12   'The main currents of English commerce were already securely established in others' hands by the time the Jews arrived in England. It is unlikely, therefore, that as merchants the Jews of Norman London ever played the economic role the Conqueror had envisioned for them ... as important conduits for the flow of silver and luxury goods into the kingdom.' (Stacey, 1995, 83)

13   There were nine self-governing Jewish communities by 1159 and around 200 Jewish settlements in total by the end of twelfth century. After 1194, Jewish moneylenders were restricted to towns with archae, and the English Jewries became concentrated in twenty-seven towns/cities (Hillaby, 2003, 16).

14   Stacey (2013, 117–127).

15   Stacey (1995, 94) has calculated that during 1241–1242 'the total wealth of the community as a whole, in bonds and chattels, must have amounted to approximately £133,333 – about a third of the total circulating coin in England at that time'.

16   In the case of the 1241–42 tallage, Stacey (1985, 175–249) found that 'more than 75% of this total tax was paid by ten individuals; more than half was paid personally by three named Jews'.

17   'Three quarters of the Jewish population eked out a living at the lower end of the urban scale. Where and when the distribution of wealth in the Jewish population can be compared with that of the urban Christian population, we find that they are remarkably similar. Anglo-Jewry was part and parcel of medieval urban society – no richer and no poorer. Around half of the Jewish population was too poor to pay taxes at all, as in the Christian community.' (Mell, 2017, 215)

18   The tradition of Jewish women working as midwives and wet-nurses goes back to ancient times. In the Book of Exodus, Pharoah's daughter hires a Hebrew wet-nurse for the baby Moses. The baby is, of course, the wet-nurse's own son.

19   Bartlet (2009, 12–14).

20 Mell (2017, 215).

21 'All the essential elements of the thirteenth century's system of moneylending by bonds against gages (pledges) were in place by the 1160s and being practiced by Christians. It is likely, indeed, that Christian lenders were the pioneers in developing them.' (Stacey, 1995, 89–90; see also Richardson, 1960, 50–82)

22 Analysis of loans by Ethan Margolis shows that 'the vast majority of lenders who lent the greatest sums of money also lent the greatest numbers of loans', (Ethan L. Margolis, 2015, 'Evidence that the Majority of Medieval English Jews were not Moneylenders, with an Emphasis on Document E', www.academia.edu/17606720/Evidence_that_the_Majority_of_Medieval_English_Jews_were_not_Moneylenders_with_an_Emphasis_on_Document_E_101_249_4).

23 'The early twelfth-century provincial Jewries share 'a suggestive combination of minting rights, proximity to important fairs, and political loyalty to King Stephen, which together point towards moneychanging and buillion dealing, accompanied by moneylending, as the primary economic determinants of Jewish settlements during this period ... As late as 1159 substantial Jewish settlements were found *only* in areas that remained under the king's control *and* where important mints or fairs were located.' (Stacey, 1995, 86–89)

24 Foreign merchants seeking to do business in England had to exchange their own currency for English coin, according to Stacey (1995, 85), who argues that, 'In the increasingly monetised local economies of eleventh-century northern Europe, moneychanging probably became an increasingly important economic activity for Jews, especially in connection with fairs where foreign merchants might often prefer silver bullion to the local specie as a medium of exchange.' (Stacey, 1995, 79–80)

25 '[T]here were no obstacles to Jews accepting silver or gold vessels in pawn, exchanging English pennies with merchants for ingots, plate, or foreign coin, or even buying up slag metal in order to refine it into silver. Like others engaged in such coinage-connected activities, Jews during Henry I's reign were probably also lending money.' (Stacey, 1995, 84)

26 Stacey (1995, 84) points out: 'Unlike the moneyers, [Jews] were not restricted to exchanging money only within their own county. They could therefore travel widely to the fairs that were springing up during Henry I's reign in Bury St Edmunds, Winchester, St Ives, and elsewhere [as they did on the continent] ... Jews could also bargain with more than one moneyer: if they disliked the price for silver offered by one, they could go to another. In so doing, they could also take advantage of fluctuations in the price of silver from one area of England to another.'

27 In 1158 Henry II dismissed the traditional moneyers and drastically reduced the number of regional mints created in Stephen's reign. 'From 1180 all foreign coin had to be exchanged and reminted through 10 royal mint-exchanges and nowhere else ... but by 1180, the balance of Jewish economic activity in England had already shifted decisively away from the combination of moneychanging, moneylending, and bullion dealing on which the Jews of Norman England had depended, toward a much more exclusive reliance upon moneylending.' (Stacey, 1995, 87–88)

28 Stacey (1995, 90).

29 'Without denying that the numerical majority of Jewish loans in England were for small sums advanced to peasants and townsmen, the fact remains that prior to 1275, the great bulk of Jewish capital in England was committed to loans of £10 or more made to the socially eminent.' (Stacey, 1995, 96)

30 The great Jewish magnates of the later twelfth century included Isaac and Abraham fils rabbi Joseph of London; Jurnet and Benedict of Norwich; Brun and Josce Quatrebuch of London; and Aaron of Lincoln. They had close ties with the major Christian moneylenders at this time, chief of which were men such as the Flemish William Cade and William Trentegeruns of Rouen, and later William Fitz Isabel, Gervase, and Henry of Cornhill (see Stacey, 1995, 89; Richardson, 1960, 50–82).

31 Stacey (1995, 90).

32 Ibid.

33 Financial records provide rich seams of information on the medieval Anglo-Jewry. In the twelfth century, the main source of information was the pipe rolls (so called because they looked like pipes when rolled up), the annual audits of the shrieval accounts at the Michaelmas exchequer. From end of the twelfth century and the whole of the thirteenth century, there is much more information available in the form of charter, fine, patent and close rolls, as well as the plea rolls of the Exchequer of the Jews (see Hillaby, in Skinner, 2003, 16–40; Stacey, in Skinner, 2003, 41–53; Bartlet, in Skinner, 2003, 113–128).

34 One of the functions of the Exchequer of the Jews by the mid-thirteenth century if not before was to control where Jews in England lived. Permission to change place of residence had to be obtained for a fee from the Exchequer (Brand, in Skinner, 2003, 73–79; see also Stacey, 2013, 106–7).

35 Richardson (1960, 115–20).

36 Paul Brand, 'Jews and the Law in England, 1275–1290', *The English Historical Review*, Vol. 115, No. 464 (Nov., 2000, 1139); Stacey (1995, 93).

37 Before the introduction of chirographs, financial transactions were recorded on strips of wood called tally sticks, a very ancient system that had been in use for around 2,000 years. Their use in the Middle Ages was ubiquitous. A tally was typically 20–30 cm in length. Notches of different widths, depths and intervals were cut to record the details of the loan. Once agreed, the tally was split lengthwise and half given to each party, their name written on each half.

38 The main purpose of the *archae* system was not to protect Jewish citizens' lives, but to keep closer tabs on Jewish money. Stacey (in Hillaby and Hillaby, 2013, 20) argues that the establishment of the *archae* from 1194 and the creation of the Exchequer of the Jews were 'less directly responses to the massacres of 1189–90 than has sometimes been suggested ... [and] are better understood as reflections of an increasingly aggressive royal claim to exercise exclusive lordship over all the Jews of the kingdom'.

39 Of 316 extant documents relating to the financial transactions of the Anglo-Norman Jews, 258 are on parchment and 58 on wooden talley sticks. Of the 258 parchment documents, 243 are chirographs. 'Hebrew Documents from Medieval England', (Judith Olszowy-Schlanger, Lecture to the Hebrew and Jewish Studies Centre, Dec 2014).

40 While Jews usually used attorneys who were relatives, they were sometimes represented in court by Christian attorneys, and vice versa.

41 'In common with the equity courts of the later fourteenth and fifteenth centuries, the Exchequer of the Jews allowed the participation of women independent from their husbands, fathers or male kin. Women were able to apply to the court whether they were single, married or widowed, and in the capacity of a daughter or mother. The Exchequer accepted pleas from married women concerning their own credit interests, and also those concerned with the credit interests of their husbands or sons.' (Hoyle, 2008, 119–129)

42 While in prison, Jews could still be visited by their Christian clients, who would have been anxious to arrange terms while the Jewish lender was still alive, in case the king appropriated the loan for himself after the lender died.

43 The top rungs of English society were unusually cash-hungry due to the structures of feudal society, which left the aristocracy and religious houses carrying a heavy financial burden. 'Ready cash was needed, often on very short notice, to pay the fines, scutages, aids and amercements demanded of them by the king.' (Stacey, 1995, 96)

44 'Nowhere else in northern Europe was there a Jewish community with so much wealth per capita, or one so completely dependent upon moneylending, as were the Jews of England in the century or so prior to 1275.' (Stacey, 1995, 93)

45 The first official statement of the Jews' special status was a charter issued by Henry II, which has not survived, but was reaffirmed by his sons Richard and John. (Richardson, 1960, 100)

46 The Angevin kings of England were part of the Plantagenet dynasty, which was descended from Geoffrey d'Anjou, Duke of Normandy from 1144–1151. The dynasty began with Henry II, who was crowned in 1154, and ended with Richard II, whose reign lasted until 1399. The term 'Angevin' refers to the first three Plantagenet monarchs: Henry II, Richard I and John. England under King John lost control of most of the Angevin territories, including Anjou. His son, Henry III, is therefore sometimes considered the first Plantagenet king.

47 This protection was affirmed by Henry II when he became king in accordance with the Laws of Edward the Confessor (Leges Edwardi Confessoris, c. 1136). The Laws stated: 'It should be known that all Jews ... ought to be under the guardianship and protection of the lord king; nor can any one of them subject himself to any wealthy person without the licence of the king, because the Jews themselves and all their possessions are the king's. But if someone detains them or their money, the king shall demand [them] as his property if he wishes and is able.' (Hillaby and Hillaby, 2013, 17)

48 After attacks on the London Jewry in 1189 and York and Lincoln Jewries in March 1190 (along with several others, such as Kings Lynn in January 1190, Norwich in February 1190, Stamford in March 1190 and Bury St Edmunds in March 1190), the Crown made strenuous efforts to reinstate loans and punish the attackers. The Charter of Liberties for the English and Norman Jews, issued by Richard I on 22 March 1190, restated the rights of the Jews 'to reside in our land freely and honourably' and their status and privileges, as well as the obligation on Christians 'to guard and defend and protect them'. King Richard's motivation, as Stacey has pointed out, had more to do with protecting his financial interests than defending his Jewish subjects (Hillaby and Hillaby, 2013, 4 & 20).

49 1194 Capitula Iudeorum 24 (Hillaby and Hillaby, 2013, 20).

50 Hillaby and Hillaby (2013, 225).

51 Hillaby and Hillaby (2013, 360).

52 Stacey, in Hillaby and Hillaby (2013, 22).

53 Roth (1941, 16); Stacey (1992, 270); see also Stacey (1987, chapters 4 and 6).

54 Regarding burial of a deceased person, the Torah (sacred Jewish law) states: 'You shall bury him the same day ... His body should not remain all night.' Jewish burials today still usually take place as soon as possible after the death.

55 This followed decrees by the Lateran Council in Rome in 1179 forbidding Jews from having Christian domestic servants, and in 1215 ruling that Jews must wear a badge on their clothing identifying them as Jewish (Hillaby and Hillaby, 2013, 47).

56 Edwards, in Skinner (2003, 91–2).

57 In the late 1260s, the Friars of the Sack in London purchased Jewish land and properties from Queen Eleanor of Provence and built themselves a church, which abutted a synagogue still in Jewish ownership. In September 1272, after the Friars complained that their Jewish neighbours were interrupting their own worship with *continuum ululatum*, Henry III confiscated the synagogue and gave it to the Friars (Hillaby, 1990-2, 101).

58 This was the wedding celebrated by the family of Aaron le Blund in Hereford (cited in Hillaby and Hillaby, 2013, 392).

59 Payments for permission not to wear the badge were paid to the Exchequer, providing useful income.

60 Hillaby and Hillaby (2013, 393).

61 Jews were frequently associated with animals and bestiality in Christian texts and imagery in the Middle Ages. In medieval bestiaries they were often depicted as owls, hyenas and fabulous creatures associated with scatological behaviour. Another expression of the medieval Christian view that Jews were morally depraved was the association of Jews with defecation (Jeffrey J. Cohen, *Hybridity, Identity and Monstrosity in Medieval Britain* (Palgrave Macmillan, 2006)). Matthew Paris, in *Chronica Majora*, relates at some length a story about one Abraham of Berkhamsted, who places a statue of the Virgin Mary in his privy so he can defecate on it daily. When his wife objects and retrieves the statue, Abraham is furious and murders her (Bale, in Skinner, 2003, 141–2).

62 'The idea of communal blame adopted in the first cases [of blood libel] ... had profound implications, for it helped prepare the way for later and eventually modern condemnations of the Jewish people.' (Rose, 2015, 237)

63 The blood libel gained 'power and resonance from typological associations between the purported victims and the Christ child, as well as from the growing cult of the Holy Innocents and the increasing popularity of miracle stories of the Virgin Mary' (Rose, 2015, 235). The Marian cult became widespread in the Middle Ages and similar representations are found in statues and stained glass in many places in Christian Europe. The biblical figure of Mary was, of course, Jewish, as was Jesus, and there is no evidence to suggest that either Jesus or his mother ever rejected Judaism. The earliest followers of Jesus were Jews and called themselves Jewish Christians. The separation of the two religions took place gradually over several centuries after the death of Jesus.

64 A *synagoga*, or ecclesia statue is on display at the east end of Winchester. The Ecclesia represents the triumph of the Church. Other famous examples of synagoga come from Stanton Fitzwarren, Southrop, and Lincoln and Rochester Cathedrals.

65 Jews in medieval England did not wear the *pileum cornatum* as far as we know, so

these depictions need some explanation. The artwork in Winchester's Holy Sepulchre Chapel is strikingly similar to work from the royal monastery of Sigena in north-eastern Spain and the great eleventh- and twelfth-century churches in northern Sicily, such as at Cefalu and Monreale. The Winchester paintings may have been done by artists from Spain or the Norman kingdom of Sicily travelling northwards in response to commissions for work. Jews were well-established in both Spain and Sicily in the Middle Ages, where the *pileum* would have been worn, as they also were in Winchester by the mid-twelfth century. It is therefore possible that the Jewish portraits in the chapel were modelled on actual people known to the artists, although not necessarily from Winchester. It is probable that Bishop Henri de Blois, returning to Winchester in around 1159 from several years' exile, commissioned the artists, having seen their work in Europe, to produce the Chapel frescoes and new sections of the Winchester Bible. The style of the paintings in the Chapel is similar to that of two of the later artists of the Winchester Bible and the paints used are of the same mix.

66 Winchester psalter 1250, f. 21r of psalter, now BL Cotton MS Nevro C iV (Elizabeth Parker in Hillaby and Hillaby, 2013, 349–50).

67 Kushner (2008, 97).

68 'The Miracle of the Jew of Bourges' tells the story of a Jewish boy whose father throws him into a heated oven after discovering he has taken holy communion, but who is saved, unharmed, by the Virgin Mary. The story was very popular and frequently depicted in the Middle Ages, linked to the myth that Jews were involved in host desecration. The depiction of the Jew of Bourges story in Winchester Cathedral dates from the sixteenth century and served to remind worshippers of the Virgin Mary's salvation from being Jewish (Kushner, 2008, 97).

69 Clanchy (2014) makes the important point that anti-French sentiment in thirteenth-century England was a response to the characteristics of Anglo-Norman lordship and completely distinct from nineteenth-century nationalism.

70 Krummel (2015).

71 'Fable 24 narrates a tale of frogs that have become angered by their king who fails to protect them and cannot articulate clear solutions for survival ... Fable 24 could very well be a warning to the English Jews not to turn away from God and not to be troubled by a silent God ... Fable 38 [about a hare and her family] moralizes that it is better not to move than to move. The moral of Fable 38 resonates with Jewish history and reminds us of the Jews' departure from Rouen in the eleventh century and the process of being too-soon unwelcome in England as evidenced by a series of ritual murder charges in the century.' (Krummel, 2015, 786–787)

72 The acrostic for the *piyyut* Who Is Like You? contains the message: 'I am Meir son of Rabbi Eliahu from the city of Norwich which is in the land of the isles called Angleterre', [ani Me'ir b'Rabi Eliahu me'medinat Norgitz asher ba'aretz ha'i hanikrat Anglatira] (Pim, 2013, 47; Einbinder, 2000, 153–59; see also Lipman, 1967).

73 'Un juif, même s'il est pauvre, s'il a dix fils, les mettra tous à l'étude des lettres, non pas pour le gain, comme le font les chrétiens, main afin qu'ils comprennent la Loi de Dieu; [il fera apprendre à lire] non seulement a ses fils mais aussi à ses filles.' (B. Smalley, *The Study of the Bible in the Middle Ages* (Indiana: Notre Dame, 1964, 78), cited in Hatot and Olszowy-Schlanger, 2018, 72). The English translation is mine.

74 Judith Olszowy-Schlanger, Hebrew Documents from Medieval England, 2014, lecture to OHJS at Oxford University 8 Dec 2014, text reproduced on OJH website http://oxfordjewishheritage.co.uk/news-events/lectures-and-special-events/316-hebrew-documents-from-medieval-england-2.

75 Jewish books were 'privately owned and privately used ... in marked contrast to Christian books, which were predominately produced and subsequently safeguarded by religious institutions' (Olszowy-Schlanger, ibid.; see also Olszowy-Schlanger, 2016).

76 Olszowy-Schlanger, in Hillaby and Hillaby (2013, 257). Sepher ha-shoam, Bodleian Library, MS Bodl. Opp 152. No. 1484.

77 See Hillaby and Hillaby (2013, 254). Manuscript containing the responsa of Moses of London, Bodleian Library, Oxford, Bod MS Mich. 502.

78 Hillaby and Hillaby (2013, 263).

79 Bartholomew Cotton, cited in Olszowy-Schlanger (2016).

80 See, for example, a bilingual Psalter in Hebrew and Latin (Cambridge, Trinity College, MS R.8.6,f.1) reproduced in Hatot and Olszowy-Schlanger (2018, 73). The Hebrew would have been copied out by Jewish scribes for Christian Hebraists. '[O]nly in England can we find tangible evidence that these interests of Christian scholars involved cooperation between Hebrew and Latin scribes.' (Malachy Beit-Arié in Hillaby and Hillaby, 2013, 70)

81 Bodleian Library, MS Bodley Or. 621, fol. 2v. (Abrams and Merchan-Hamann, 2020, 8–9). Illustrated on page 6.

82 Bodleian Library, MS Bodley. Or. 621. For this and other examples of Hebrew manuscripts from medieval England see Judith Olszowy-Schlanger, *Les Manuscrits hébreux dans l'Angleterre mediévale: étude historique et paléographique* (Paris: Louvain, 2003).

83 Condemned to exile in 1290, the precious libraries of books belonging to the Jews of Huntingdon and Stamford in Cambridgeshire were put up for sale. Many were bought at bargain rates by a Benedictine monk called Prior Gregory of Ramsey Abbey, who studied them exhaustively and used them to create a unique Hebrew/French/Latin dictionary, known as the Longleat House Dictionary (Longleat House, MS 21 ff.29–143). See Judith Olszowy-Schlanger (2008) *Dictionnaire hébreu-latin-français de la Bible hébraïque de l'Abbaye de Ramsey (XIIIe s.)* Ramsey Abbey in the Fens (founded in 966) was a major centre of scholarship with a phenomenal Hebrew library, which was ransacked during the dissolution of the monasteries in Henry VIII's reign. The dictionary was stolen from Ramsey Abbey by Robert Wakefield, a keen sixteenth-century Hebraist, who became the first lecturer in Hebrew at Cambridge University. Wakefield drew on his knowledge of Hebrew scripture when he was tasked with helping Henry VIII build a case for divorcing his first wife. In the seventeenth century, the dictionary was acquired by William Laud, Archbishop of Canterbury and Chancellor of Oxford University (see Hillaby and Hillaby, 2013, 318).

84 Further evidence of friendly relations between Jews and Christians can be found in the pipe rolls, which document several instances of Jews giving possessions to Christian neighbours for safekeeping in times of danger, not always wisely as it turned out, since these were cases in which the Jewish owners tried unsuccessfully to retrieve their belongings.

85 Both Christ Church Cathedral and St Augustine's Abbey in Canterbury were clients of the Jewry and leased urban plots to the Jews. When Aaron of Lincoln died in 1186, Baldwin owed him £150.

86 Christians and Jews in Norman England were mutually hostile to intermarriage. A Christian deacon in Oxford who converted to Judaism and married a Jewess was burned at the stake in 1222 for having 'sex with an animal'. (Maitland, F. W., 'The Deacon and the Jewess; or, Apostasy at Common Law', *Jewish Historical Society of England* 6 (1908–1910), 260–276)

87 As Paul Brand points out legislation became the vehicle for imposing 'special restrictions and regulations' on the Jewish community in the thirteenth century, with new laws relating exclusively to the Jews being introduced at least once or twice in every decade from 1218 on. Brand (2000, 1139–1140)

88 Winchester ranked fourth in wealth amongst English cities in 1066, after London, York and Norwich, and equal to Lincoln. In the early twelfth century, it was about equal to Norwich after London, and above York and Lincoln, and by the second half of the century it appears to have ranked between fourth and eighth in wealth among English towns (Thomas, E. et al., 'Royal and Mercantile Centre: 1066–1300', in Derek Keene, *Survey of Medieval Winchester* (Oxford University Press, 1985), 44).

89 The new Norman castle measured 4.5 hectares or 11 acres in total. The redesigned royal palace was 'second in neither quality or quantity to the palace of London', according to Gerald of Wales, (op. cit). The new cathedral, begun by Bishop Walkelin in 1079 and completed in the 1120s, covered 5,750 square metres (62,000 square feet) and was 'the largest church in Western Europe except for St Hugh's abbey church at Cluny ... The nave was almost exactly as long as the Constantinian Basilica of St Peter's in Rome.' (Edward Thomas, Martin Biddle and Francis M. Morris, 'Royal and Mercantile Centre: 1066–1300', in Keene, 1985, 38–40)

90 After the civil war between Stephen and Matilda in the mid-twelfth century, Winchester's bishop, Henry of Blois, who was Stephen's brother, submitted to Queen Matilda and excommunicated his brother in return for complete control over religious appointments in England. When Queen Matilda went back on this agreement, Henry realigned with Stephen and his queen. When the forces of Queen Matilda attacked Winchester, Henry set fire to the royal palace and fled to Wolvesey Palace, where he was besieged as the city burned.

91 Many high-ranking bishops from other towns owned or rented property in Winchester, a clear measure of its ecclesiastical importance (Thomas et al., in Keene, 1985, 41).

92 Winchester's economy was hit hard from 1204 by Philip II's conquest of Normandy, which meant the valuable overseas market dried up. The city was besieged twice by the French during the First Barons' War in 1216–17, and many people fled. Winchester fell sharply in the ranking of English towns during these years, but remained one of the most prosperous cities in England.

93 Winchester was a 'rival to London in some respects as late as 1269' (Thomas et al., in Keene, 1985, 46).

94 Thomas et al., in Keene (1985, 45, footnote 93).

95 Vincent (1996, 9) points out that des Roches performed the same service for Henry III from 1231, with disastrous results for the Jewry.

96 King John died in 1216 and his nine-year-old son Henry was crowned later that same month. As he had not yet come of age, he was placed under the guardianship of William Marshall and Peter des Roches. Henry was crowned a second time, in May 1220, but only assumed formal control of his government in 1227. Before then and for several years after, he was heavily reliant on his closest advisors. His chief ministers at this time were Hubert de Burgh and Peter des Roches, although the two men were political rivals. De Burgh fell from favour in 1232, and des Roches in 1234. Henry ruled his kingdom from this time on (Carpenter, 2004, 312–338).

97 Not Poitiers, according to Vincent (1996).

98 Vincent (1996, 9) describes him as 'a courtier of genius'. For word play on des Roches's name see Vincent (1996, 3–4).

99 During his years out of royal favour in England, des Roches became a key advisor to Frederick II, the Holy Roman Emperor, who he accompanied on Crusade from 1227. He was in Palestine to witness the Treaty of Jaffa in 1229, which restored Jerusalem to the Christians, and in 1235 he fought on the side of Pope Gregory IX and Frederick III against the Roman commune.

100 The bishop's Soke effectively divided land ownership in Winchester in two, with most land owned either by the Church or the Crown, and each run by a steward or bailiff who answered either to the king or to the bishop.

101 Des Roches was not alone in squeezing out landholders in this way. Many monastic houses and cathedrals in the twelfth and thirteenth century expanded their lands by this same method.

102 Vincent (1996, 177–179).

103 Jews were listed at living on Scowrtenestret by 1148. In the thirteenth century the street was also called Yeruestret and vicus Judeorum. It was officially named Jewry Street post expulsion (Kushner, 2008, 56–60; Hillaby and Hillaby, 2013, 394).

104 Thomas et al., in Keene (1985, 40–41).

105 The first ghetto in Europe was established in Venice in 1516 on the site of an old iron foundry, 'ghetto' being the Italian word for 'foundry'. The site's distinctive physical feature was that it was gated and could be sealed off from the rest of the city. Many European towns and cities in the Middle Ages had Jewish streets and Jewish districts, which were turned into ghettos at times of Jewish persecution. The ghetto, as Krummel (2015, 776) puts it, thus 'figures as the antithesis of free movement and civic independence'.

106 The 1275 Statutes of Jewry stated: '... the King granteth unto them [the Jews] that they ... may have intercourse with Christians, in order to carry on lawful Trade by selling and buying. But that no Christian, for this Cause or any other, shall dwell among them.' ['Mes ke par cest encheson ne per autre nul Crestien ne seit couchant ne levaunt entre eus'] (cited in Krummel, 2015, 777–778).

107 Study of Torah and Talmud, the two most sacred texts in Judaism, had been central to Jewish life for many centuries. Torah is the first five books of the Bible, which were written in the form still used today between the sixth and fifth centuries BCE. Talmud is a collection of the discussions and interpretations of Torah by the early rabbis and sages, written down over several centuries and completed between the third and fifth centuries CE.

108   Unlike the Mediterranean Jews of southern France, many of whom were Sephardi, the Jews of of Northern France, known in the Middle Ages as Tsarfat, were closely linked to the Rhineland Jews of Worms, Speyer and Mainz and were Ashkenazi. When they came to England in the eleventh century, they brought the religious rites of the Ashekanizim with them. In modern Hebrew the word *Tsarfat* refers to all the Jews of France. I am indebted to Pam Manix for this information.

109   Deed of sale for Nottingham house, 28 June 1257 from Exchequer of the Jews, London, Westminster Abbey Muniments, No. 6799. The property was sold by Judith fille de Menaham and her husband Yedidyah ben Elazar to Jacob ben Menaham ha-Vardimasi. (Reproduced in Hatot and Olszowy-Schlanger, 2018, 86–87)

110   Some of the wealthiest of the London Jews seem to have had private synagogues inside their houses. (Hillaby and Hillaby, 2013, 354–355)

111   Throughout the Jewish world, the provision of a synagogue was a civic and spiritual duty for the leading members of a medieval Jewish community.

112   Hillaby and Hillaby (2013, 356).

113   Hillaby J. and Sermon R., 'Jacob's Well, Bristol: Mikveh or Bet Tohorah?', *Transactions of the Bristol and Gloucestershire Archaeological Society*, 122 (2004), 127–152.

114   Benedict Crespin's *mikveh* was discovered on the site of his house in Milk Street, London when the site was excavated in 2002. His *mikveh* was 'beautifully constructed from green sandstone brought from Kent, the joints fitting so closely that they were watertight, and it had steps going down to the water' (Bartlet, 2009, 69; see also I. Blair et al., 'The Discovery of Two Medieval Mikva'ot in London and a Reinterpretation of the Bristol Mikveh', *Jewish Historical Studies*, 27 (2002), 32–34).

115   Prior to the expulsion, the Jewish community paid the Priory of St Swithun's eight shillings a year for the lease of the land. By the time of the expulsion in 1290 a considerable sum was still owing in rent arrears.

116   I am indebted to Hester Abrams for her comments on the rite of *tahara* (ritual preparation of the dead for burial).

117   Hillaby and Hillaby (2013, 55).

118   Ibid.

119   Winchester, Northampton and Bury St Edmunds were all sites of important fairs as well as royal mints. Fairs were profitable for the bishops who owned them, who may have favoured Jewish money changers over their Christian competitors. 'If Jews offered more favourable rates of exchange on foreign silver than did their Christian competitors, it would be clearly to the advantage of fair owners like the abbot of Bury St Edmunds or the bishop of Winchester to encourage Jews to attend their fairs. Jews in turn might well find particularly attractive fairs … whose owners also held the minting-rights, and so could control the price his moneyers would pay for silver.' (Stacey, 1995, 85–87)

120   Described as 'the finest surviving aisled hall of the thirteenth century' by Thomas et al., in Keene (1985, 45, footnote 92).

121   In the previous century, the 1159 *donum* placed the Winchester Jewry fourth-equal with Cambridge. In the Northampton Promissum in 1194, it ranked seventh in the country. The tallages for 1221, 1223 and 1226 placed the Winchester Jewry in third place after London and York. In the 1241 tallage, Winchester had fallen to tenth place,

and in the 1255 tallage it had risen to first place, equal with Lincoln.

122   Thomas et al., in Keene (1985, 41).

123   The skeletons of fifty-four children, fifteen adolescents and three adults were analysed and revealed evidence of rickets in children, but also of well-healed fractures, suggesting medical skills of the Jewish community (Kushner, 2008, 107).

124   Bartlet, in Skinner (2003, 122).

125   Analysis of skeletons from York's Jewish cemetery found that rickets and TB were the same in both Jewish and Christian children, but anaemia and child mortality were lower in Jewish infants. York was one of the wealthiest Jewish communities until 1190, so better health and longevity may have reflected the local situation rather than the national one (Kushner, 2008, 107).

126   'The combination of organic residue analysis, site excavation and animal and fish bone evidence was consistent with the presence of Jewish houses in eleventh- and twelfth-century St Aldates, Oxford, hitherto only suspected through documentary information. This is the first identification of specific religious dietary practices using lipid residue analysis, verifying that, at least 800 years ago, medieval Jewish Oxford communities practised dietary laws known as Kashruth.' (Dunne, J., et al., 'Finding Oxford's Medieval Jewry Using Organic Residue Analysis, Faunal Records and Historical Documents', *Archaeological and Anthropological Sciences*, 13/48 (2021). https://doi.org/10.1007/s12520-021-01282-8)

127   Jewish women in medieval England do not all appear to have worn *sheitls* (wigs worn by Orthodox married Jewish women). One case in the records concerns an attack on a pregnant Jewish woman called Bessa in 1244, whose assailants dragged her to the ground by her hair. The assailants, it should be noted, were Jewish in this case. Bessa, the pregnant wife of Elias of Warwick, was beaten up by Leo, his wife Henna, his daughters Anterra and Sigge, and his sister Muriel. Bessa miscarried, and the whole family was exiled from Warwick for life (see Ruben, A., *The History of Jewish Costume* (London, 1973), 95; Kisch, G., 'The Yellow Badge in History', *Historia Judaica*, 4 (1942), 95–144).

128   Bartlet, in Skinner (2003, 120).

129   Abrams (2017, 117–126).

130   Latin and French had taken over from Anglo-Saxon after the Norman Conquest; by the thirteenth century Latin was embedded as the language of administration, church and law; French as the language of the court and literature (see Clanchy, 2014, 258–259).

131   Kushner (2008, 107).

132   Anglo-Norman Jewish names do not tell us where an individual was born. The toponym, i.e. 'of Winchester', or 'of Canterbury', refers to a person's main place of business, not their birth, and could therefore change over a person's lifetime. Jews also had Hebrew names, which often, but not always, record who they were the son, daughter or wife of, e.g. Manasser fils Josce, or Jacob ben Judah of London.

133   Bartlet (2009, 22).

134   Baskin (1991, 94–114).

135   Minting had stopped in 1180, but was revived in 1205–07, 1217 and 1248–50. Abraham of Kent may have been attracted to Winchester by the 1217 revival and the financial and business opportunities it opened up.

136   In 1225, Henry III came of age. He was embroiled that year in fall-out from the First Barons' War, skirmishes with rebellious forces in Wales and the imminent threat of losing Gascony to the French. This was also the year in which he signed and sealed the new version of the Magna Carta and the Charter of the Forest, in large part a peace settlement with England's rebellious barons.

137   Close rolls for 1234. The standard Latin formulation used for widows was *que fuit uxor* ('who was the wife of') or *vidua* ('widow') (Bartlet, in Skinner, 2003, 118).

138   The 1234 Close Rolls record the king relieving Hugh Sangaver of interest on a £10 loan from Licoricia of Winchester and Peytavin of Winchester (Bartlet, 2009, 42).

139   Close Rolls 1234 (cited in Bartlet, 2009, 21).

140   'By the thirteenth century, there were a total of forty-one English Jewish women "dealing in loans or associated transactions" independent of men.' (Bartlet, 2000, 46) From the twelfth century, Jewish women were lending to Christians, travelling from one place to another to deal with financial matters and to protect their financial interests. By the thirteenth century, Jewish women were 'a visible presence' in the pipe rolls (Bartlet, 2003, 113; Krummel, 2015, 798–790).

141   Hoyle (2008, 119–129).

142   Bartlet (2000, 31–54).

143   Bartlet (2009, 29).

144   Kushner (2008, 87).

145   Bartlet (2009, 44).

146   Vincent (1996, 288–289). Vincent also makes the point that Abraham Pinche's local unpopularity may have been rooted in his financial activities, along with his mother Chera Pinche. Both were exploited by Peter des Roches between 1231 and 1234 into 'persuading their debtors to part with land for his new religious foundations at Selborne and Titchfield'.

147   According to Vincent (1992), Pinche may have lost des Roches's favour just when he needed it most. Des Roches had returned from Crusade in 1231 and needed to raise money to pay for Henry III's unsuccessful incursions in northern France and to assert his own authority in Winchester and beyond. If Vincent is correct in his analysis, by 1235 Pinche may have been a victim of a deliberate 'programme of anti-Jewish (financial) and antisemitic (demonising) measures instituted by des Roches' (Bale, in Skinner, 2003, 135; Vincent, N., 'Jews, Poitevins, and the Bishop of Winchester', in D. Wood, ed., *Christianity and Judaism* (SCH 29, Oxford 1996), 119–132).

148   A few months after her husband's death, Belia and her brother-in-law Elias – another of Chera's sons – joined forces with Licoricia to make a loan of 18 marks to one Roberto de Bello Alneto. Not long after this, Belia succeeded in buying back properties that Deulebene had held in fee before his death.

149   Medieval Jewish women are frequently named as joint owners of houses and land, and as owning property in their own right. After 1271 this may have been a way to get round the ruling that Jews were only allowed to own property that they either lived in themselves or rented to other Jews. If a widow remarried, she was expected to return the house that she had shared with her husband to his children, which sometimes led to disputes with sons and step-sons after a husband died.

150   Bartlet (2009, 26).

151   David is known to have worked with Benedict Crespin on numerous occasions.

In 1238, David, Benedict Crespin and Aaron of York were ordered to maintain Simon the Crossbowman, a servant of the king's and probably a Jewish convert. In 1238, David and Benedict Crespin were two of eight Jews who conducted an enquiry into coin-clipping.

152   Bartlet (2009, 56, footnote 38).

153   Ibid.

154   Genesis 30:13.

155   In the worsening conditions of the 1260s many Jewish moneylenders were forced to sell loans secured on land. Walter de Merton acquired the land for his college by buying several such loans (Stacey, 2013, 118–119).

156   A bond dated June 1244 from Barons of the Exchequer to Henry III gives remission concerning a bond of the lady Eleanor, the king's sister, for £100 owed to David the Jew of Oxford. David died in February 1244 and Licoricia was in the Tower of London when this remission was granted.

157   The Deputy Keeper of the Records, Public Record Office, ed., Close Rolls of the Reign of Henry III, A.D. 1237–1242, 345–47. The English translation is Stacey's (see Stacey, 1985, 189).

158   Bartlet (2009, 69).

159   Henry III founded a Domus Conversorum in Chancery Lane, London in January 1232 on the site of one the Jews' main London synagogues (now the site of King's College Library), which he had expropriated for this purpose and without any form of compensation. Converted Jews lived in the quasi-monastic Domus and received a weekly stipend while they were learning their new faith (Stacey, 1992, 263–283).

160   Stacey (1995, 97).

161   Bartlet (2009, 65).

162   Bartlet (2009, 72–74).

163   In 1250, Henry III granted Licoricia 'seisin of all lands, rents and tenements late of Thomas de Cherlecot, which are in her pledge, and that she shall not be disseised thereof til the debts for which they are pledged were paid or until she be disseised thereof by judgment of the courts' (Pat. R. Henry III, 1247–1258, 58, cited in Bartlet, 2009, 73–74).

164   According to Stacey (2003, 41), the Worcester Parliament of 1241 revealed that the English Jewry 'controlled approximately 200,000 marks in liquidable assets, a sum equivalent to roughly one third of the total circulating coin in the kingdom'

165   'Between 1240 and 1255, the government derived approximately ten percent of its ordinary annual revenues from the direct taxation of the English Jewish community, even though Jews, as we have seen, represented no more than one-tenth of one per-cent of the total English population. Jews, in other words, paid taxation at a rate one hundred times greater than if they had contributed to the king's coffers in proportion to their numbers. By 1255, these huge taxes had drained away most of the capital upon which Jewish moneylending depended. With so little money left in Jewish hands to lend, Jews had little prospect of recovering their losses through new loans, even after 1255, when the burden of taxation eased.' (Stacey, 2013, 118)

166   Based the calculations of Stacey (1995, 95). See also Stacey (1987). For total Jew-ish taxation during the same period, see Stacey (1985, 135).

167   Stacey (2003, 51).

168   The first mention of Cokerel's financial dealings is in 1245.

169   Reference E210/284 at the National Archives.

170   Reference E210/5408 at the National Archives.

171   Bartlet (2009, 83).

172   Benedict also acquired a large country estate in the Sutton Hundreds, which in addition to the main house came with thirty-nine acres of pasture and parklands, as well as the cottage, possessions and land of the unfortunate estate tenant, a widow called, somewhat appropriately, Eva Broke (Bartlet, 2009, 94).

173   Keene (1985).

174   Pat R. Henry III, 1266–1172, 223, dated 5 May 1268.

175   Bartlet (2009, 95).

176   This was one route by which royal courtiers acquired land at the expense of other Christians. Jews were forced to sell 'existing loans to other lenders, often for mere pennies on the pound. The purchasers of these loans were usually Christians, often royal courtiers or members of the king's own family, who bought them in order to acquire possession of the lands that the Christian borrowers had pledged as security for their loans.' (Stacey, 2013, 118–119)

177   From the chronicle of Arnold Fitz-Thedmar, cited in Hillaby and Hillaby (2013, 228).

178   Even Robert Grosseteste conceded that the Jews were more lenient moneylenders than the French Cahorsins. The chronicler Matthew Paris quoted him as saying, 'If you make a loan of a hundred marks with £100 to be paid back at the end of the year, they will not receive less than £100. On the other hand when you return money to a Jew he has lent you, he will receive it with good grace and with interest only commensurate with the time it has been lent.' (Hillaby and Hillaby, 2013, 179–180)

179   Robert of Gloucester, *Chronicles*, quoted in V. W. Page, ed., *Victoria History of the Counties of England: Hampshire and the Isle of Wight* (London: Constable, 1912), 310. See also Bartlet (2009, 92, note 6).

180   Belia and her son Jacob were lending to high-ranking noblemen and clergy by this time, including the Earl of Gloucester and the Archdeacon of York. The Earl of Gloucester led the ransacking of the Canterbury Jewry in 1264 but, just four years later, Belia sold the same earl bonds worth 1,000 marks, an indication perhaps of the straitened circumstances of both parties in the aftermath of the Barons' War.

181   Hillaby and Hillaby (2013, 49); Bartlet (2009, 90–92).

182   Belia's second widowhood left her in financial difficulties, according to Bartlet (2009, 91–92). She had trouble raising the fine of 725 marks to keep two-thirds of Pictavin's bonds, and had still not paid it ten years later. The year after Pictavin's death in 1261, she had to take action against two Jews, Isaac and his brother Bonenfaunt, for stealing from her, paying a large sum to have them banned from Bedford for five years.

183   H.G. Jenkinson, ed., Calendar of the Plea Rolls of the Exchequer of the Jews, AD 1275–1279 III, (London 1929), 227, in Berman Brown and McCartney (2004, 18).

184   H.G. Jenkinson (1929, 73), in Berman Brown and McCartney *Jewish Historical Studies*, 39 (2004, 18).

185   I am indebted to Robert Stacey for his explanation of fee rents.

186   Brand (2000, 1141–2).

187   The 1275 Statute of Jewry also tightened up social controls of the Jewish population, with new restrictions on where they were allowed to live, who they were allowed to rent or give their property to, the reissue of existing bans on employing Christian servants, and the enforcement of the wearing of the badge.

188   Stacey (1995, 99–100). Mundill (1998, 1–21) argues that commodity brokering became a principal occupation for some Jews. See also Mundill (1991, 137–170), cited in Stacey (1995, 99).

189   Brand (2000, 1142-3).

190   Bartlet (2009, 109–112).

191   Brown and McCartney, 'David of Oxford & Licoricia of Winchester', *Jewish Historical Studies* 39 (2004, 18).

192   Another Jewish woman, Pucelle, widow of Bonavye of Newbury, was murdered in Winchester in the same year as Licoricia.

193   S. Cohen, ed., *Calendar of the Plea Rolls of the Exchequer of the Jews, AD 1277–79 V*, (London, 1992), 98, cited in Brown and McCartney (2004, 19).

194   Zefirah Rokeah, 'Crime and the Jews in Late Thirteenth Century England: Some Cases and Comments', *Hebrew Union College Annual*, 55 (1984), 134.

195   Mundill, 'Edward I and the Final Phase of Anglo-Jewry', in Skinner (2003, 61–62).

196   Zefira Rokeah, 'Money and the Hangman in Late-13th-Century England', *Jewish Historical Studies*, xxxi (1988–90, 83–109)

197   Brand (2000, 1149–52).

198   Bartlet (2009, 134).

199   Hillaby and Hillaby (2013, 397).

200   Hillaby and Hillaby (2013, 48) state that Jacob survived for another ten years and inherited the two Bedford houses belonging to his parents, but was hanged in 1285 on charges of fraud.

201   Bartlet (2009, 136).

202   Paul Brand cites several documents to support his argument that Henry acted as an *agent provocateur* in this undercover operation against his former co-religionists. A book of the king's wardrobe expenditure for 1277–8 (PRO, C 47/4/1) mentions that Henry of Winchester was travelling the country buying 'melted silver' for the treasury, for which he was paid the generous sum of £8 in expenses. While about this business, Henry was arrested by the overzealous constable of Bristol for being in possession of suspect goods 'to the value of 300 marks and 'plates' to the value of 200 marks' (PRO SC 8/218, no 10892) and duly locked up in Bristol castle. Henry was subsequently reimbursed on the king's authority for the costs incurred during his imprisonment. A second payment was made for Henry of Winchester's additional expenses 'for gifts and bribes given both to Jews and Christians to convict them of exchanging'. Brand (2000, 1149–53).

203   Brand (2000, 1152–53).

204   Patent Rolls, 1279, 320, A. E. Bland an M.C.B. Dawes, eds, Calendar of Fine Rolls I (22 vols) (London 1911), 144, cited in Brown and McCartney (2004, 23).

205   Robert C. Stacey, '1240–1260: A Watershed in Anglo-Jewish Relations?' *Historical Research*, 61 (1988, 135–150).

206   Ibid.

207 Henry III confiscated at least three London synagogues and part of the Oxford Jewish cemetery between 1231 and 1272, reassigning them to Christian religious houses. In addition to the creation of the *Domus Conversorum* in 1232, he also provided buildings, land and materials for Christian religious houses in Jewish neighbourhoods, probably placed there with a view to converting Jews to Christianity (Stacey, 2013, 121–122).

208 There were an estimated 300 Jewish converts out of a Jewish population of around 5,000 at the peak periods of conversion during Henry III's reign (see Krummel, 2015, 784; Stacey, 1992, 269; Mundill, 1998, 256; Lipman 1967, 36–37). There is evidence that the king financially supported converts and their families, and he intervened in several legal cases to enforce payments to converted Jews. Henry also took a close interest in individual conversions, attended the baptisms of numerous converts, in several cases acting as godfather to the newly converted (Stacey, 1992, 269).

209 Stacey (2013, 120–127) positions Henry III as a regrettable trailblazer in this regard: 'Henry III was a member of the first generation of European kings to see such conversions as even conceivably a part of their royal responsibilities. And no other thirteenth-century king, including St. Louis of France, took this responsibility as seriously as did Henry III.' See also Stacey (1992, 263–283).

210 'Mary's bodily integrity, epitomized by her perpetual virginity and her bodily assumption into heaven, were seen as proofs of the Church's triumph over the Jews who had crucified her son, and who continued to crucify him through their assaults on innocent Christian children ... Devotion to the Virgin Mary thus became a central theme in tales of religiously-motivated Jewish murder and ritual crucifixion from the thirteenth century on.' (Stacey, 2013, 127) For more on Henry III's Marian piety, see Nicholas Vincent, 'King Henry III and the Blessed Virgin Mary', in *The Church and Mary*, ed. R. N. Swanson, *Studies in Church History*, 39 (Woodbridge: Boydell, 2004, 126–146).

211 According to the chroniclers, Henry went in person to Lincoln to hear Copin's confession, and having done so, immediately overturned Copin's 'plea bargain' and ordered his execution. According to Stacey (2013, 126): 'The chroniclers are also unanimous in reporting that Henry was the driving force in prosecuting the case thereafter. Ultimately, some ninety Jews were arrested, of whom nineteen were executed: Copin in Lincoln, and eighteen others in London, who were dragged and hanged after Christmas. The remaining seventy-one Jews were also condemned to death by the king and his great men meeting over Easter at Reading, but these Jews were ultimately freed through the intervention of the Dominicans, the Franciscans, or Richard of Cornwall (the sources differ).' See also Gavin Langmuir, 'The Knight's Tale of Young Hugh of Lincoln', *Speculum*, 47 (1972), 459–482, reprinted in Langmuir's volume of collected essays, *Toward a Definition of Antisemitism* (Berkeley: University of California Press, 1990).

212 Bartlet (2009, 122 and 141).

213 Brand (2000, 1154–56). The unfinished draft was copied into another document in around 1300, now in the British Library, BL. Add.MS 32085. See also Rigg, cited in Mundill (1998, 295-8).

214 Brand (2000, 1138-1158)

215 Bartlet (2009, 138).

216 Ibid.

217 Bartlet (2009, 140).

218 Hillaby and Hillaby (2013, 396–397).

219 Bartlet (2009, 137).

220 The importance of observing the Sabbath is a constant refrain in the Bible from Genesis on, with the destruction of the first temple and the sufferings of the Jewish people routinely ascribed by the biblical prophets to the people's failure to observe the Sabbath (see Isaiah 58:13–14; Jeremiah 17:19–27; Ezekiel 20:10–22; Nehemiah 13:15–22).

221 Huscroft (2006, 156–157).

222 Charles II, King of Sicily, expelled all Jews from Maine and Anjou in the Edict of Expulsion on 8 December 1289 (Mundill, 1998, 282–283).

223 Huscroft (2006, 156–157).

224 Bernard Leeman, 'The 1290 AD Massacre of the Jews at Jury's Gap Romney Marsh', Rye Library Archives. See also Mundill (1998, 255).

225 Christian taxpayers in England paid the king a tax of £115,000 in 1290 to secure the expulsion of the Jews. Stacey (1995, 100; 1993, 9–25) asserts that 'Politics, propaganda and myth are much more directly involved in this extraordinary decision than is economics.'

226 E.M. Rose, 'Why Were the Jews Expelled from England (1290)?' paper delivered at the *American Historical Association*, January, 2021.

227 Bale, in Skinner (2003, 133). See also Jeremy Cohen, *The Friars and the Jews: The Evolution of Medieval Anti-semitism* (Ithaca, 1982)

228 E.M. Rose, 'Edward and the Eleanors – Royal Piety and the Expulsion of the Jews from England (1290)', paper delivered at the *Medieval Academy of America*, March, 2021 (forthcoming in print 2022).

229 Pim (2013).

230 Pim (2013, 30–37).

231 Hillaby and Hillaby (2013, 140–141).

232 Mundill (2010, 259).

233 Bartholomew Cotton, cited in Olszowy-Schlanger (2016).

234 There was no equivalent in medieval England to the genocidal racial ideology underpinning Nazism, but the deployment of punitive and exclusionary legislation had the deliberate effect in both countries of making daily life for Jews increasingly unsustainable.

235 'To describe such individuals, let alone the community as a whole, as powerful, is to fail to understand the marginal and at best tolerated status of Jews in medieval England.' (Kushner, 2008, 93)

236 Kushner (2008, 93).

237 This is Alter's gloss of the final line of the *eshet chayil*. Alter translates the line as 'Give her from the fruit of her hands, and let her deeds praise her in the gates.' (Alter, 2018, 31)

Index